THE PRIVATE EYE ANNUAL 2004

EDITED BY IAN HISLOP

"I've never worried much about global warming until now"

Published in Great Britain by
Private Eye Productions Ltd
6 Carlisle Street, London W1D 5BN

© 2004 Pressdram Ltd
ISBN 1 901784 34 7
Designed by Bridget Tisdall
Printed in England by
Goodman Baylis Ltd, Worcester

2 4 6 8 10 9 7 5 3 1

THE PRIVATE EYE ANNUAL 2004

EDITED BY IAN HISLOP

HUTTON INQUIRY

KEY WITNESSES RECALLED

DAY 994

AS LORD Hutton's inquiry neared its conclusion, a number of key witnesses were recalled to be questioned by top barrister Andrew Bandicoot QC.

First into the box was the enigmatic, taciturn, supremely confident Sir Scarlett Pimpernel, head of JIF (the Joint Intelligent Farrago).

Sir Scarlett had previously told the inquiry that he had been personally responsible for every detail of the dossier, published by No. 10 Downing Street on 21 September 2002, entitled *Saddam Is Going To Launch Nuclear Rockets And Poison Gas At London In 45 Minutes Unless We Do Whatever President Bush Says* (HMSO, £45).

Sir Coldicream: Sir Pimpernel, I draw your attention to this e-mail, dated 18 September, from the Chief of Staff at Number 10, Jonathan Powermad. It says, as you will see... *(rummages through several thousand files for some hours before locating the incriminating electronic message in question)*... "To Pimpernel from Powermad, urgent. We have a bit of a problem with paragraph 7143 of the dossier. Where it says 'Saddam has no weapons', we feel the word 'no' should be replaced with the words 'lots of'. This is, of course, entirely up to you, but the PM would be very grateful if you could see your way to underwriting the necessary amendment (as would your friend Alastair!)!"

Do you remember receiving this email?

Sir Scarlett: I believe that this is an accurate appraisal of the information available to me at this moment.

Sir Carrycot: Does it not contradict your previous evidence that Number 10 had no hand whatever in the final wording of the dossier?

Sir Scarlet-face: ...er ...um ...that remains my position. I see no contradiction between my previous statement and the exact opposite.

Sir Callcentre: And yet, Sir Redface, when we look at the dossier we find that the very changes urged on you by Mr Powermad were incorporated in the final version. Are you suggesting that this is to be attributed to mere coincidence?

Sir Pumpernickel: On the contrary, the changes were made entirely on my own initiative, following my receipt of new intelligence from a top secret source, namely Mr Powermad at Number 10.

Campbell Diaries Reveal Concern Over BBC Man

AMONG new evidence supplied to the inquiry yesterday was an edited version of the diaries of Mr Alastair Campbell.

Monday June 7
Meeting with TB and GH. We agree we can use Kelly to f*** Gilligan. Then we can use Gilligan to f*** Kelly. Then we can use both of them to f*** the BBC. Then everyone will be f***ed except us. TB f***ing pleased.

Tuesday June 8
F***!!! F***ing Kelly has f***ed up at the Committee. He was meant to f*** Gilligan, but instead he f***ed us, the stupid f***er.

Saturday June 12
The sad death of Dr Kelly has robbed the nation of its finest and most dedicated public servants. I am deeply distressed by this tragic news, as are TB and GH.

PS. This diary is available to the highest bidder. Only offers in the region of £5 million or above will be considered.

Campbell's Four-Letter Word Shock

Spin!

THE FUCK STOPS HERE
ALASTAIR CAMPBELL

LATE HUTTON INQUIRY NEWS

NEW documents released by the Hutton Inquiry have revealed that Dr David Kelly played a key role in the outing of Dr David Kelly as the key source for reports from Andrew Gilligan and Susan Watts.

"Apparently it had something to do with him meeting journalists in his lunch break every day, instead of going to Pret à Manger to buy a sandwich and then going back and eating it at his desk" said a stunned… *(cont'd p. 94)*

Film Choice

HIGH HOON

TCM **1.45 am**

CLASSIC cowboy movie where the embattled lawman is waiting to see if he is going to be hanged for turning over Doc Kelly to the gang of vicious journalists. Deserted and doomed, what can he do? Features the haunting theme tune 'Do not forsake me Alistair Darling'.

Nursery Rhymes Revisited

There was a young man called Andrew Gilligan
He worked for the Beeb, but I don't think he
will again,
No more beans for him to spill again,
Poor old Andrew Gilligan (begin again?).

IS THIS THE REAL LORD LUCAN?

IN WHAT is probably the most astonishing scoop the world has seen for decades, Private Eye can reveal that the fugitive peer Lord Lucan has been tracked down to a small office in London's docklands.

For years, it turns out, the missing Earl has been hiding out in the *Sunday Telegraph*, assuming the identity of a leading journalist.

This amazing claim is made in a new book by one of Britain's most respected policemen, the former Inspector 'Knacker of the Yard' Knacker, entitled *'I Made All This Up'* (Conman Press £7.99).

In the book, Knacker describes how he received a tip-off from a reputable drug-dealer, who gave him a photograph of Dominic Lawson which proved beyond any doubt that Lawson and Lucan were one and the same.

Unlucky Lawson

Beyond the startling physical resemblances, other parallels between the two men are too numerous to be mere coincidence:

- Their names both begin with the letter 'L'
- They both had fathers who were Lords
- They both have right-wing views
- Both of them went to Eton
- Both had moustaches, except one of them.

But the biggest giveaway of all is that Lucan, in his assumed persona as a journalist, went out of his way to publish an absurd story claiming that the real Lucan had become a hippy in Goa, in order to put the world off the scent.

Lucan Latest
WIFE DISMISSES LAWSON STORY

LADY LUCAN today dismissed the Lawson story as "complete and utter nonsense".

"My husband," she said, "was an Englishman of the old school. He would never have stooped so low as to end up editing the *Sunday Telegraph*."

Letter to the Editor

Dear Sir,

Those of us who knew 'Bungle Dommy' laughed and laughed when we read your story about how he is meant to be Lord Lucan.

I had the pleasure of knowing 'Dommy' well when he was editing the Spectator, in those far-off days of the swinging Nineties.

We all used to hang out at a little club called 'the Garrick' – me, Dommy, Chazza Moore, Hugh Fearnley-Whittingstall and Borrie Johnson.

Dommy was the life-and-soul of the party, always up for another bottle of claret or seconds of steak-and-kidney. How anyone could think of Dommy murdering his nanny in cold blood and then running away utterly beats me.

Yours,

ALEX CHANCELLOR,
Tuscany.

NEXT WEEK

IS THIS THE REAL SHERGAR?

ALL THE evidence suggests that this fugitive aristocrat is none other than the missing racehorse Shergar.

The broad, noble forehead, the flared nostrils, the shirt and tie can only point to one conclusion. We are so desperate we'll run anything.

IS THIS THE REAL SADDAM HUSSEIN?

STARTLING new evidence has emerged which suggests that the man they call 'Jungle Osama' may in fact be the fugitive dictator Saddam Hussein.

The moustache, the beard and the fact that he promises "death to the west" surely *(That's enough. Ed.)*

The Tale Of The Three Blairs

ONCE upon a time, there was a big, bad, lifestyle guru who turned up outside the brick house where the three Blairs lived. There was Daddy Blair, Mummy Blair and little Leo Blair. "Mrs Blair," cried the big, bad, former topless model. "Mrs Blair, please let me in. I have a new lipstick that will make you look really pretty. And a shirt for you, Mr Blair, that won't show the sweat under your arms."

But the three Blairs hid under the table and pretended not to be in.

Then the big, bad New Age enthusiast got very angry and said, "I'll huff and I'll puff and I'll blow the gaffe on you!".

"Ooh!" cried Daddy Blair,

"I'm really scared. Tell her to go away."

But this just made the big, bad, former mistress of the Australian conman even more determined to get into the house.

"I'm going to blow you all away," she screamed, "with my new book which I'm going to sell for millions of pounds."

"No, no," cried all the Blairs together. "We won't let you in. Not by the hairs on Mr Blunkett's chinny-chin-chin."

Then the big, bad daughter of the mad, psychic soothsayer climbed down the chimney in her wolf-skin tracksuit and gobbled them all up because they had forgotten to light the fire. © *Madonna 2003.*

"The novelty's worn off, I'm afraid. They should just cut him down now"

What You Didn't Bother To Read Because You've Read It All Before

'MY NAUGHTY NIGHTS WITH TOP PLAYWRIGHT HAROLD PINTER'

By Joan Bonkwell

Chapter One

I SHALL never forget the time I first met Harold Pinter, the world's most brilliant writer and nor will you because you've read about it so often.

Harold dazzled me with his menacing silences and his incredible way with words:

"I want *(pause)* to *(pause)* be on Late Night Line-Up *(pause)* with you," he said.

How could I resist? Within minutes we were engaged in passionate discussions about his latest play.

We couldn't stop ourselves, even though both Harold and I were married and we were both incredibly boring *(cont. p. 94)*

Tomorrow: How I hated being called 'The Thinking Man's Crumpet'.

Extracted from *'The Thinking Man's Crumpet – The Joan Bonkwell Story'* by Joan Bonkwell *(BBC Press £18.99)*

A Tank Driver Writes

Each week a well-known tank driver is invited to give his views on the Middle Eastern situation.

THIS WEEK: **Ari Sharon** (Tank No. PZ 742X)

That Arafat, guv?! It's all his fault, this crisis, innit? Why isn't he stopping it? What's he up to? Bugger all – excuse my Hebrew – that's what!!

Do you know what I'd do with that Arafat, if I had my way (which I do)?

I'd train a special squad of Mossad hitmen to go over the wall (which we've built) and string him up!! It's the only language he understands.

I had that Barbara Amiel in the back of the tank once. Wonderful looking woman for her age...

Reprinted from the Jerusalem edition of Tanks & Tankmen *(prop. Lord Black of Crossfire).*

What You Missed

THE STEPHEN FRY DIARIES

Thurs 24 October

Buttocky bummy bums with double arses! The Deutsche ZeeberNeu Bank promised to come up with a bridging loan to the NFCG who had agreed to part fund the venture capital requirement for 'Bright Young Things'... oh bum bum arsety bum!

Tomorrow: Sodding bottoms bum arses! My film gets made.

© *Sir Crispin Dry, The Sunday Telegraph 2003.*

I feel a bit of a prick

CROWD TURN ON MASTER ILLUSIONIST

By Our Political Staff **The Great Andrew Marrvo**

THERE WERE ugly scenes yesterday as America's favourite magician, Tony Blaine, became the focus of unwelcome attention from the British people.

As he dangled by a thread high over everyone's heads, he was pelted with eggs and jeered by raucous onlookers.

Over-Egged

"Wake up and do something," cried the crowd, bored by Blaine's inactivity and his concentration on surviving for the next 44 days.

Security men tried to stop protestors, but were unable to prevent a barrage of abuse targeted at David Blair.

Said a spokesman for David Blair, "This wouldn't happen in America where Tony was put on a pedestal by cheering supporters.

"Over there they think he is marvellous. What is wrong with you guys?"

POLLY FILLER

EXCUSE ME for asking, but what exactly is so remarkable about David Blaine?

A man sits around doing nothing for 44 days and expects everyone to applaud him. Ring any bells, girls? Remind you of anyone you live with?

I mentioned this to the useless Simon but couldn't elicit any response due to the fact that he was slumped in front of the television watching 24-hour coverage of David Blaine (!) on the Sky Extreme Boredom Channel with continuous commentary from Paul Ross and expert opinion from A.A. Gill!

And I see that David Blaine is wearing a nappy. Doesn't that just say it all? Men are **all** big babies with exhibitionist tendencies.

I was tempted, on behalf of the women in Britain, to go and throw an egg at him!

But if he's anything like the useless Simon, he wouldn't know what to do with an egg! He would probably put it in the microwave, just like he did with toddler Charlie's wet football boots, which resulted in the kitchen catching fire!

Needless to say, the hopeless new Liberian au pair panicked and threw the goldfish bowl over the flames, thus killing Moby! (My amusing name for the fish, by the way – Charlie wanted to call him "Fishy"!)

Honestly, these girls. You would have thought that coming from Monrovia she would have seen the odd house on fire recently and would know what to do! But not a bit of it!

ANYWAY, Mr Blaine, when you come down from lying around in your silly box, if you want to see something truly amazing, come and watch me performing the incredible daily balancing act on the tightrope of career and motherhood!

Now that *is* magic!
© *Polly Filler*

HUMPTY DUMPSTER TO RETIRE

HUMPTY DUMPSTER, the legendary egg-about-town, is to step down from his wall which he has occupied contin-uously for the last thirty years.

"The familiar figure of Dumpster sitting on the wall seemed an integral part of our lives," said his friend No one, "but recently he has taken to falling off the wall and has ended up in pieces." Said another, "He is a shell of his former self. He is a broken man. There's too much egg on his face."

The Butcher, The Dacre, The Candlestick Maker

However, Dumpster insisted that he had jumped from the wall rather than be pushed by Paul Dacre.

"Anyone who says I didn't choose to go in my own time is talking complete rubbish and should be given my job immediately."

■ **Gingerbread House Prices To Fall – New Shock** ■ **Does Eating Curds And Whey Give You Cancer?** ■ **Why Asylum-seeking Jumblies Should Be Sent Home In A Sieve**

Clarke To End 'Blatant Bias' In University Entrance

by Our Education Staff *Lunchtime O'Level*

THE EDUCATION Secretary Charles Clarke today announced plans to make entrance to universities much fairer.

University Challenged

"It's time we put everyone on a level playing field," he said. "At the moment preference is given to bright children who pass exams."

From now on, under Mr Clarke's plan, universities will no longer be allowed to discriminate on the grounds of intelligence or academic ability.

Mr Clarke plans a new regulatory body, Offswot, to ensure that the more able pupils are not over-represented in Britain's tertiary education sector.

"We look forward to the day," he said, "when everyone in the entire country goes to Oxbridge and comes out with a First."

"Gap year kids, I expect"

TORY IN SECRETARY SCANDAL

What's in my diary this week, darling?

You're going to be sacked

Wedding of the Century
How They Are Related

MONEY
|
Ben Goldsmith

MONEY
|
The Hon. Kate Rothschild

RED FLAG TO RETURN TO CONFERENCE

by Our Man In Bournemouth **TUC Biscuit**

THE traditional anthem of the socialist movement is to be reintroduced for this year's Labour Party Conference. In recent years, the great anthem, sung to the tune of Tannenbaum, has been thought to be too redolent of the old class-conscious Labour Party.

Now, by popular demand, the Red Flag is back and delegates will be given a special song sheet so that they get the words right.

Those Words In Full

♫ *"The working class can kiss my arse, I've got the PM's job at last."* ♫

© *T. Blair.*

KENNEDY'S TIME HAS COME

Are they open yet?

GLENDA SLAGG

FLEET STREET'S TERMINATOR!?! SHE'LL BE BACK!! (UNFORTUNATELY)

■ SCHWARZENEGGER!!? Arnie-tchasickofhim?! (Geddit?!) Just 'cause he's got muscles the size of melons, this hulking hunk from the land of Hitler thinks he has a god-given right to go round a-grabbin' and a-gropin' the gals!?! What a disgrace!?!?! They should terminate him before he rapes every woman in California!? Come on, Dubya – put him on Death Row before it's too late!!

■ ARNIE – don'tchaluvhim?!? He gets MY vote?!?! With his muscles the size of melons, this handsome hunk from the land of the Blue Danube is just what California needs!?!! OK, so he flirts with the gals but what hot-blooded bimbo wouldn't mind Arnie a-humpin' and a-pumpin' his iron round at her place!?!? (Geddit?!) California here I come!?! Yessiree!?!?

■ HATS OFF to 17-year-old soccer wonderboy Wayne Rooney?!? This have-a-go hero restored England's pride by punching a Turkish footballer in the tunnel – and for why?!? 'Cos he insulted Becks!!?! Come on, Mr Blair – give him the OBE now!?!?!

■ WAYNE ROONEY?!?! Doesn't he make you ashamed to be putting on an England shirt and flying the flag of St George from your white transit van as you have a few beers and run over a toddler *(Is this right? Ed.)* This overpaid soccer thug decided to take the law into his own hands by thumping up some Turkish player when the cameras weren't looking!?!? Give him the boot, Sven, preferably in the face like Fergie and Becks – remember?!?

■ *SEEN* Kill Bill*?!? Me too... Z-z-z-z-z-z-z-z-z-z-z-z-z-z-z-z-z-z-z--z-z-z-z-z-z-z-z-z!?!?!?*

■ HERE THEY ARE – Glenda's Fall Guys!!! (Geddit?!?)

● **Oliver Letwin** – I'd like to go on a desert island far, far away with you, big boy!?!?!

● **Charles Moore** – The *Telegraph*'s Lord Snooty!?!? OK, he's been given the sack – well, I've got a sack you can slip into any time, Charlie?!?!?!

● **John Paul II** – OK, you didn't get the Nobel Peace Prize!?!? Fancy coming round for a bit of consolation?!?!?! Know what I mean?!? You're my Pope Idol!!?! Geddit?!?!

Byeeee!!!

MANDY FOR EU JOB?

I know all about corruption

THEN AND NOW

Governor of California 1966   Governor of California 2003

Here's one for the Gipper

Here's one for the Groper

IDIOTS ELECT CELEB

by Our Political Staff
Holly Wood

NO ONE was surprised last night when a celebrity was elected Governor of California by a large majority of idiots.

Said one idiot, "I have seen the celebrity on video blowing things up which makes him the obvious choice to manage the economy of California."

Making his inaugural address, the celebrity said, "Vere iss my script?" as the crowd cheered.

He later promised women reporters that "Mine vill be a hands-on administration."

Celeb 117,638,433
Politicians 0

Poetry Corner
with Sir Trevor Barbados

The Burial Of Sir Charles Moore
by Conrad Black

AS A BOY in Trinidad, I was taught to recite this poem about the end of one of Britain's greatest heroes, who had just won a great victory in the circulation war against the Times (1996-2003).

It seemed to sum up the British attitude to being sacked in a wonderfully inspiring way.

Not a drum was heard, not a funeral note,
As the message came through from Lord Black.
There on the screen was the email he wrote –
"Clear your desk, Moore, you've just got the sack."

Young Moore's face turned as white as a funeral shroud,
And a tear slipped down from his eye.
"That's jolly unfair!" he cried aloud,
"Pray, what is the reason why?"

"The answer is simple, my dear Mr Moore,"
Came back the reply from his boss.
"The sales of our paper have gone through the floor,
And your pages are brim-full of dross."

Moore gasped and then sobbed and then stifled a sigh
As he vanished away in the night.
With his crumpled plus-fours and egg-stained school tie,
Poor Charles was a pitiful sight.

What on earth could he say, if asked by a hack?
What excuse could he possibly hatch?
"I know – I'll say that it wasn't the sack.
I had to leave because I had this tremendously important book to finish about Mrs Thatch."

9

EU OFFICIAL NOT GUILTY OF FRAUD

by Our Brussels Staff Phil Pockets

BRUSSELS was reeling last night after a shock new report revealed that an unnamed Luxembourg official working in the Paperclip Directorate of the European Commission had never committed a single corrupt or fraudulent act during his ten years working in Brussels.

There were no "holes in his accounts". He had never "skimmed a contract". He had never appointed his brother-in-law's mistress to a single EU post.

EU Commissioners immediately called for his dismissal.

Said the EU's top fraud expert, Neil Kinnochio, "This is totally, utterly and utterly, totally outrageous. After all the good work that we have been doing to preserve the EU's reputation, along comes just one rotten apple like this, and the rest of us *(Cont. p. 94)*

"We have your daughter – she'll be released when you come and finish our extension"

THAT BUSH FAST FOOD MEAL IN FULL

Giant Whoppa with Lies and an Oil Sheik (to go)

Results Of BBC's 'Big Watch' Surprise No One

by Our Literary Staff **T.V. Tie-In**

THE BBC's historic nationwide competition to find the most popular film or video of a book which no one has read last night came to its climax, when 21 books which have been turned into a film or TV serial in the last 12 months fought it out for the title of the nation's favourite video.

The winner, to universal amazement, was the hitherto-unknown *Best Of The Teletubbies (surely 'Lord of the Rings'? Ed).*

That 'Big Watch' List In Full

1. **Inspector Morse** (The Box Set)
2. **Best Of Poirot** (now also on DVD)
3. **Of Mice And Men Behaving Badly**
4. **To Kill A Mockingbirds Of A Feather**
5. **East Of Enders** by John Steinbeck
6. **The Complete Big Brother** by George Orwell
7. **Tender Is The Newsnight**
8. **Gone With The Wind In The Willows**
9. **How Clean Is Your Bleak House?**
10. **Lord Of The Lies** by Jeffrey Archer

(That's enough top books. Ed.)

Escaped Kidnapped Briton Has Two Attractive Sisters

THERE was joy today throughout the Daily Telegraph office after it became clear that the British backpacker who escaped from kidnappers in Colombia has two attractive sisters.

"This is a story of incredible courage, bravery and, more importantly, two very pretty girls," said a beaming Charles Moore.

"This makes this story the most important front page news we've run since all those pictures of attractive seventeen-year-old girls in crop tops receiving their A Level results."

"You say slave trader – I say investor in people"

KNACKER FURY AT BBC RACISM FILM

by our Police Staff **Lunchtime O'Blues**

INSPECTOR KNACKER, Assistant Deputy Chief Inspector of the Neasden Police Force, condemned the five police recruits who were shown making racist remarks in a BBC undercover investigation yesterday.

"These men have behaved in an unforgivable way. There are always some black sheep in any family, which is why we are getting rid of them, the black bastards."

Late News

INSPECTOR Knacker is retiring from the force as of this minute. A spokesman said, "This is a black day for the police and we don't want those sort of days around here."

Even Later News

A POLICE spokesman is also retiring from his position with immediate effect. When asked for a statement his replacement replied, "No blacks, I mean comment."
(That's enough of this piece. Ed.)

AN APOLOGY
Northern Ireland

THIS MORNING, in common with all other newspapers, we may unwittingly have predicted that today was the day when the troubles in Northern Ireland would finally come to an end, and Mr Blair would be going to Belfast to announce the dawn of a new age of peace and prosperity, when Unionists and Republicans would be openly embracing one another with tears of joy, and old-age terrorists (surely 'pensioners'? Ed.) would be dancing in the streets. Headlines such as '1000 Years of Bloodshed Come To An End', 'Peacemaker Tony's Greatest Triumph' and 'Eire We Go, Eire We Go' may have given the impression that we in some way believed 10 Downing Street when they last night handed us a press release suggesting all the above headlines.

We now realise, in the light of what actually happened, that there was never the slightest chance that Mr David Trimble and Mr Gerry Adams would agree in any way about anything other than to continue the same old hopeless stalemate that has characterised the politics of Northern Ireland for as along as anyone can remember.

We apologise for any confusion that this may have caused to our readers, and any disappointment that they may have suffered as a result of believing the nonsense that we print on the instructions of 10 Downing Street.

MILLIONS WEEP AS COUGHCORDE IS GROUNDED

by Phil Aerospace

ONE of the great white hopes of British uselessness Iain Duncan Cough was finally laid to rest today.

With his sleek bald head Iain Duncan Cough had been hailed as one of the great British inventions.

But after two years of trials the backroom boffins finally admitted defeat and acknowledged that Cough would never get off the ground.

Boom & Bust

One expert who tried desperately to get him to take off said: "The problem was the noise. He didn't make any at all. Nobody was woken up."

CRUISE OF A LIFETIME TURNS TO HORROR

by Our Nautical Staff
Samuel Taylor Cholera

WHAT should have been a fun-filled voyage of discovery last night became a living nightmare as all the passengers on a cruise ship fell ill and died.

Said the sole survivor, an Ancient Mariner, "It must have been something we ate – probably the albatross which was on the menu for dinner."

"It was a real shame when everyone dropped dead because I'd been looking forward to this holiday for years."

Phew Water Water Everywhere!

"But instead of eating at the captain's table I ended up surrounded by rotting corpses as the ship drifted aimlessly around the Mediterranean."

Added the Mariner, "It really is the last time I travel with P&O."

MICHAEL PORTILLO

Are you keen on spoons?

Well, there was a time of course when I simply did not have the time for spoons, and now that my life has changed I find myself having to reassess my whole attitude to spoons – and may I add not just spoons. Knifes, forks and even ladles are all things to which I hope to devote more attention in the future.

Are you saying that politics stopped you developing an attitude towards spoons?

That's a very good point. You can get very much bogged down in party politics and lose sight of the things that really matter – like spoons. There's no way I could go back to the front bench now that I've had a chance to go round the country and see for myself just what sort of spoons ordinary people find relevant to their lives.

Did making the TV programme "Spoon Swap" alter your views in any way?

I think it's fair to say "Yes". It was fantastic to have to stir my tea with a dirty old plastic spoon from Woolworths whilst watching the other people trying to come to terms with my Spanish spoon created by Los Spoonos in Toledo. It was humbling really.

Do you think Michael Howard is a spoon man?

I think you'd have to ask Michael that. I hope that he's going to be more open to a whole raft of spoons, rather than just the narrow old-fashioned range of spoons that did so much to damage us in the public's eyes.

Will we be seeing more of your spoons on television?

Well it's early days but I am in talks with a number of production companies about new TV shows – one idea is for me to present a show where I go into celebrities' houses and you have to guess who the celebrity is by looking at their spoons.

Has anything amusing ever happened to you in connection with a spoon?

I think that was a long time ago and we've all moved on from that sort of thing.

NEXT WEEK: Sir Michael Peat – "Me and My Peat."

FOOTBALL IN CRISIS

A Special 24-Page Eye Investigation Into What's Gone Wrong

With The Beautiful Game

THE Sun SAYS

Top commentators give their view

The Barbarians At The Gate

by Brian R. Sewell

(Winner of the Peregrine Worsthorne Best Essay Award 2001)

WHAT could be more disagreeable than the idea of eleven sweaty members of the working classes, probably high on drugs and certainly grotesquely overpaid, being held up as some kind of role models in our sadly disintegrating culture?

The idea that these totally uncouth and unattractive young men, scarcely more than adolescents, and all of them pitifully ill-educated, should be allowed to run amok in the hotels of Park Lane, is obscene. Why should these testosterone-fuelled youths take it as their god-given right to emulate the worst excesses of the barbarian hordes, as so memorably depicted in the recently restored masterpiece *The Rape of Bruges* by The Master of Keown, currently on show at the *(cont'd. p. 94)*

The Posh Boys Are Worse

says Johann Sparti

(Winner of the Jayson Blair Best Essay Award 2001)

HOW typical of the media to focus solely on the members of the underclass.

When I was at Cambridge, the entire city was terrorised by upper-class Hooray Henrys who spent their time swilling champagne and snorting coke before going out into the streets to beat up local working-class youths and rape innocent townswomen before throwing them into the river where they all drowned.

Yet this was dismissed as no more than "youthful hi-jinks" and "under-graduate high spirits".

Truly there is one law for the rich, and another for the poor footballers who *(cont'd. p. 94)*

Snob Yobs

by Polly Technic

(now the University of Polly Toynbee)

THE disgusting behaviour of the Premier League foot-ballers has shocked the nation.

But what about the revolting behaviour of all those old Etonians like Prince Harry, Lord Frederick Windsor, Tom Parker-Bowles and Charles Moore? *(Are you sure about this? Ed.)* Why aren't they under arrest for rape and murder too?

And why has Eton not been closed down on the grounds of failing to *(That's enough. Ed.)*

WHAT on earth has happened to our national sport? Why oh why has football sunk so low?

The answer is simple. There is too much money washing around in the hands of young men who haven't a clue what to do with it.

And what is the source of this obscene shower of wealth which has corrupted and degraded the once-beautiful game that Britain gave the world?

It does not take a rocket scientist to work out who is to blame.

Step forward BSkyB, and its evil owner. *(You're fired. R.W.)*

Who has turned these yobs into heroes? Who has given them the licence to be obsessed with sex and money?

It does not take a rocket scientist to work out who is to blame.

Step forward Britain's gutter press, led by the worst offender of all, the Sun newspaper. *(You're fired again. R.W.)*

"I think bringing football to the island has been our greatest achievement"

THAT PREMIERSHIP TEAM IN FULL

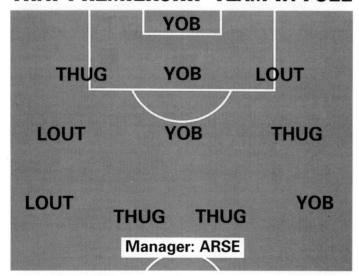

YOB

THUG   YOB   LOUT

LOUT   YOB   THUG

LOUT   YOB

THUG   THUG

Manager: ARSE

MATCH ⚽ OF THE DAY

Lineker: And joining me in the studio for a bit of expert analysis is Inspector Knacker of the Serious Crime Squad. Inspector, how do you feel it's going so far?

Knacker: Well, Gary, we're still very much hoping the lads will get a result.

Lineker: Do you think it will go to penalties?

Knacker: Well, it's too early to say, Gary, but it's an open gaol and we're looking to put seven away.

Lineker: I suppose it's all about getting players into the box...

Knacker: ...yes, Gary, once they're in the witness box, we can break through the defence and put them in the back of the van.

Lineker: Thank you, Inspector Knacker. And if you don't want to hear anything about football ever again, look away now.

Next Week: DNA Match of the Day with the Chief Pathologist

DISGUSTING SCENES IN HOTEL SHOCK THE NATION

by Our Political Staff **Peter O'Bore**

WE CAN reveal that a group of some of Britain's best-known and most highly-paid Conservative politicians were last week involved in a three-day orgy of abuse in one of the most prestigious hotels in Blackpool.

The victim of this "outrageous and horrifying" attack could not be named, although it is believed that he was Iain Duncan Cough, an innocent, 57-year-old party leader, who had earlier checked in under the name of "Mr Smith".

Appalling

Hotel staff claim that they witnessed a number of well known Tories "drinking heavily" in the hotel's George Best Bar, before going upstairs to give Mr Cough a "roasting".

Friends of the men involved deny the claims that anything untoward had happened in the hotel.

"He was asking for it," said one senior Shadow Cabinet minister last night, "by being so useless and pathetic.

"He knew what sort of people he was mixing with, and he knew we weren't in Blackpool just for a party conference."

But this latest outrage is only the latest in a long line of sordid incidents which in recent years have brought the name of Britain's once 'beautiful Party' into the gutter.

Repulsive

In 1990, an elderly woman was savagely mugged by two of the stars of the day, Mike Heseltine and Geoff Howe, and never recovered from the injuries they suffered.

In 1997, hundreds of screaming Tories viciously set upon a pathetic South London man with glasses, again claiming that he had "asked for it" with his cones hot-line.

A young Yorkshire boy suffered the same fate in 2001, pleading that he never wanted "to live through anything like this again".

But none of these tragic victims have been so humiliatingly treated as Iain *(cont'd. p. 94)*

(cont'd. p. 94)

BROWN'S DAY OF JOY

Tony's been taken to hospital

Gordon's Baby

You choose the name! Simply pick which you think is the most appropriate and ring Eye Brown Baby Line 0800 23456 (calls charged at £10 per minute. Length of average call 20 minutes)

- [ ] Nye
- [ ] Keir
- [ ] Clement
- [ ] Ramsay
- [ ] Herbert Morrison
- [ ] Chuter Ede
- [ ] John Smith
- [ ] NOT TONY

A Doctor Writes

Supraventricular Tachycardia

AS A DOCTOR I am often asked "Doctor, would you write us 2,000 words on Tony Blair by lunchtime?" The simple answer is "Yes, of course. How much money are you offering?"

What happens is that the doctor's pulse begins to race at the thought of the cash, causing an outbreak of palpitations and a rush of blood to the head. This may feel like a heart attack. The doctor, however, then immediately uses an electronic device known as "Google" which quickly calms him down by downloading all the medical information he needs to solve his article problem.

After a short rest, the doctor is ready to write another piece about John Smith, Michael Heseltine, Winston Churchill or anyone else in the news with a medical condition.

If you are worried about not making money out of *Supraventricular Tachycardia*, then you should consult an editor at once.

© A Doctor

DAILY MAIL – SHOCK REPORT

How Tony Blair has aged

Blair in 1997

Blair yesterday

THE Gnome SAYS

SIX YEARS after the death of Princess Diana in a Paris car accident, evil toady butler Paul Burrell has released letters in which the Princess claimed that people were planning to kill her in a fake car crash.

We believe that Paul Burrell should now face charges for withholding these letters for so long.

The letters should, of course, have been handed over some years ago to the Editor here at the Gnome so that we could have upped our circulation by publishing them as we hailed Burrell as a true British hero.

By choosing not to do this, Paul Burrell has perverted the course of tabloid justice, and revealed himself to be beneath contempt.

Long may he rot in a prison cell!

TRAITOR HELD

Anything you say will be taken down…

…and printed in the Daily Mirror

NEW DIANA LETTER SENSATION

AN amazing letter from Princess Diana to royal butler Paul Burrell is published exclusively by the Daily Moron today.

It proves not only that Diana predicted a conspiracy to murder her butler but that she was a devoted reader of the Daily Moron and *(cont'd. p. 2-94)*

That letter

The Mirror is a great Paper and Piers Moron is honestly really dishy!!. Yah!! After they have fixed my brakes so I die in a car accident I hope you will dish the dirt in the Daily Moron and fill your boots

lots of love

Diana XX

P.S. After I die take anything you want and hide it under your bed.

OUTRAGE AS BUTLER SELLS STORY

by our Valet Staff **P.G. Woofter**

THE BUTLER at the centre of a 'tell-all book' was branded a disgrace yesterday by his former employer, Mr Bertie Wooster, who was depicted in the best-selling book *What-Ho Jeeves!* as an upper-class twit incapable of forming attachments with women and terrified of his elderly relatives.

Said Bertie Windsor, "It's a pretty poor show when a chap can't grow a moustache or buy a hat without his bally butler telling the whole world all about it."

Continued Mr Windsor, "I mean, I'm made to look a complete nincompoop who can't even choose his own socks let alone a wife without the assistance of Jeeves." When asked for a comment Jeeves remarked, "Very good, Sir."

Tomorrow: *The night that Mr Wooster stole a silver cow creamer and I had to cover it all up.*

HEIR OF SORROWS

by Dame Sylvie Krin

(long-listed 78th for this year's Man Booker Prize)

THE STORY SO FAR: Charles's relationship with Camilla is slowly winning acceptance from the British people, much to Charles's pleasure. Now read on...

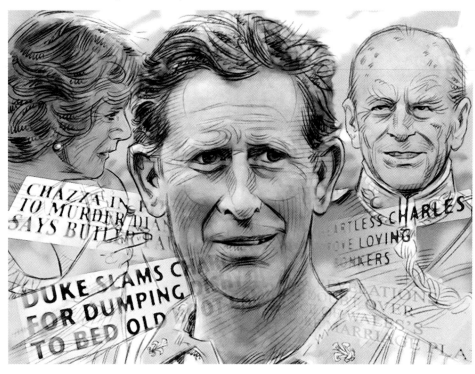

CHARLES sat in the breakfast room at Highgrove as the October sunshine flooded in through the elegant neo-Georgian windows, designed by his friend Sir Wogan Terry.

It had truly been an Indian Summer to remember. And was it too much to hope for that he too could now be granted an Indian Summer in his own life?

With a confidence he hadn't felt for years, he stirred a spoonful of organic sweetener into his cup of Lapdancer Souchong breakfast tea, and added a dash of skimmed milk from the prize-winning Aberdeen Angus Ogilvy dairy herd that he could see grazing on their GM-free pastures in the park outside.

Yes, perhaps after all things were at last looking up. What was it his old friend and mentor Sir Laurens van der Post used to say on their long walks through the Kalahari Krishna game reserve? "There'll be bluebirds over the white cliffs of Dover, tomorrow just you wait and see..."?

How very true that was, he mused.

But suddenly his reverie was broken by a loud thump as a hefty pile of newspapers was roughly slammed down on the table in front of him, spilling the pot of Duchy Original Extra-Thick Royal Crab Apple Jelly all over his Trescothick and Vaughan velvet non-smoking jacket.

"Er, Camilla, old thing – you're up! Something wrong?"

"Yes, there bloody well is, Charles!" The world's most famous consort could barely contain her rage as she held out a selection of Britain's most avidly read tabloid newspapers a few inches from his nose.

The headlines spoke for themselves.

'CHAZZA IN PLOT TO MURDER DIANA, SAYS BUTLER PAUL!' screamed one.

'HEARTLESS CHARLES DROVE LOVING DI BONKERS!' shouted another.

'ROYAL REVELATIONS CAST DOUBT OVER PRINCE OF WALES'S FUTURE MARRIAGE PLANS' yelled a thoughtful front-page editorial in the *Financial Times.*

But Camilla saved the worst of these hurtful headlines until last – 'DUKE SLAMS CHARLES FOR DUMPING DISHY DI TO BED OLD BOOT CAMILLA!'

"What are you going to do about this one, Charles?" she seethed.

There was an ominous silence as he began to take in the full horror of what must have happened.

That bloody butler of Diana's... a new book... letters from everyone... this was the worst nightmare yet... even his father was betraying him all over the pages of the *Daily Thingie* and the *Whatsit.*

Camilla angrily lit up a cigarette and blew a thick cloud of noxious smoke directly into her partner's face – something she knew he detested more than anything in the world.

"I demand an apology to be printed on the front page of every newspaper in the land!" she stormed.

"Your father has publicly insulted me in the most hurtful possible way."

"But... er... you know... it was only a very private letter, written to Diana. And it's hardly his fault if, you know..."

But his outraged paramour was in no mood to listen to his faltering remonstrations.

"Look what it says here. According to your beastly, big-mouthed father, you must have been off your trolley to hitch yourself up with a woman who makes the rear end of an average London bus look like an attractive proposition."

Charles cringed at the only too familiar nautical bluntness with which his father had made his position clear.

"You're a bloody fool, Charles!" How often had he heard those words ringing down the years...

"YOU'RE a bloody fool, Charles! What do you mean – 'an apology'?" The gruff bark of the Duke of Edinburgh boomed down the line, just as it had once done from the quarterdeck of HMS Genghis Khan, prompting several terrified midshipmen to throw themselves overboard into the frozen Atlantic wastes.

Charles was beginning to regret that he had submitted to his mistress's imperious demands rather than following his instinct to let sleeping dogs – or, indeed, dukes – lie, and let the whole thing kind of blow over.

"The person who should be apologising, Charles, is *you,* for making such a total pig's ear of your whole bloody life. Do you realise your mother'll have to rule for another 50 years now, thanks to your shenanigans with Old Bootface..."

As his father continued his admonition in similar vein for some hours, Charles found his thoughts beginning to wander.

He saw in his mind his father in the driving seat of one of his carriage-thingies, trotting quietly along with his friend the 59th Duke of Onslow, when... oh no... what's happening? ... the horses seem to be bolting and the brakes seem to have failed... and what's that? A white Fiat Uno coming round the corner...

(To be continued)

NATION STUNNED BY COUNT'S MAKEOVER

by Our Political Staff **Doris Karloff**

AWESTRUCK reporters were today invited into the castle of the once-notorious Count Dracula, to meet the man who has just emerged from one of the most dramatic makeovers of modern times.

Gone were the cobwebs, the bats and the creepy organ music.

Gone too was the coffin in which he liked to take a quick afternoon nap in the days when he was Home Secretary.

The Count too has changed his looks from the days when his protruding teeth, deathly white skin and hypnotic eyes terrified TV audiences all over Transylvania.

The Count has dispensed with his black cloak and silver-topped cane.

He now sports rimless spectacles and jeans, and smiles affably as he welcomes his journalist guests.

"Hi," he says. "I'm Michael Howard. I'm a regular kind of vampire. Can I offer you a glass of blood?"

"He means coffee," laughs his stunningly beautiful former '60s model wife, as she hands round a selection of delicious, chocolate-covered bat nibbles.

"People have got the wrong idea about me," says the Count. "All that stuff about bloodsucking and being nasty to Ann Widdecombe – it's all in the past.

"The world has changed since the 15th century when I was last in power under Thatch The Impaler – and I've changed with it."

"We in the modern Vampire Party have to be inclusive, caring, compassionate and ready to listen to what the villagers are saying.

"Please excuse me," the Count smiled, "but I have to leave you now, as the sun is coming up and I've got a meeting in the crypt."

Before

After

What You Will Not Read in the Sun

THE Sun SAYS

Time to live in the 21st century

IT MAY have been alright for the Middle Ages, but frankly, in the world of 2003 the old-fashioned hereditary principle looks as out of place as spats and a top hat.

The idea that someone could expect to take over the job just because his Dad was the King of the Castle before him is rightly viewed as obscene.

There is no other word for it.

Obscene

Today we do not need a world in which we are expected to bow the knee to some spoiled brat for the sole reason that he happened to be born into the right family at the right time.

This is the kind of fawning old-school tie snobbery that has strangled this country for centuries, making it the laughing stock of the world.

What we want and expect is a Britain in which the only thing which counts is talent, merit and ability, the three 'T's.

We deplore the decision of Her Majesty the Queen to nominate Prince Charles for the most important job in British life just because he is her son.

The Sun Says – Wake up Your Maj and give the job to James Murdoch!

ALL THIS AND MORE IN BRITAIN'S FAVOURITE FAMILY PAPER!!!
(the family in question being that of Mr Murdoch)

"We are what we eat, Brian"

TORY PARTY RECOVERS FROM NASTY COUGH

by Our Political Staff **Benny Lin, Meg O'Zone, T.C.P. Linctus, E.U. Calyptus** and **Lady Covonia Syrup**

THE CONSERVATIVE Party, which for months has been on its deathbed with a seemingly terminal Cough, has made a miraculous recovery.

Cough-In

The Cough, which threatened to end the Party's life, has now completely disappeared after emergency treatment by Dr Acula, the distinguished Transylvanian specialist.

Mr Iain Duncan Cough, who came from nowhere to become a successor to such titans as Winston Churchill, Margaret Thatcher and John Major, was known as "The Quiet Man" for his oratorical technique of saying nothing at all, punctuated by the occasional nervous cough to indicate to his followers that he was still there. Now he isn't.

Our Medical Correspondent DR UTTERFRAUD on what happens when a political party recovers from a nasty Cough.

IN THE initial stages, the patient experiences an extraordinary feeling of euphoria as the miseries of living with the Cough wear off.

The patient feels healthy, fit and ready for anything. Sadly, however, this sense of elation is short-lived, and the patient soon returns to its former debilitated *(cont'd p. 94)*

Blair's Top Ex-Spin Doctor **ALASTAIR CAMPBELL** joins the Eye's team to offer his unique insights into Britain's political scene. Read him today.

WHY MICHAEL HOWARD HASN'T GOT A FUCKING HOPE

I'VE got some advice for you, Four Eyes. Fuck off.

© World copyright A. Campbell 2003.

THIS WEEK

NO. 94
MICHAEL HOWARD

How would a Tory government's approach to spoons be different from that of the present government?

That is a very intelligent question and it requires a proper answer.

Can I have it then?

Well, we have to move towards the kind of society where the government doesn't tell you what sort of spoon you can or can't have. We need to provide choice, and the obvious way to do this is through Spoon Vouchers. I believe people are fed up with the nanny state approach to spoons.

How would your new system work?

That is another very good question, if I may say so. And it highlights the very point I'm making.

Which is what?

Well, let me try to explain. If I want an expensive spoon for my children, I should be allowed to provide such a spoon without being penalised for doing so. So under our Voucher System I could exchange the voucher for half the value of the spoon and make up the rest from personal savings. Doesn't that seem fair?

But what about people at the bottom end of the earnings scale, who may not have the money to benefit from such a system?

Well that's your best question yet, if I may say so! I believe very strongly that no one in our society should be deprived of access to spoons, but the best way to achieve that is to work towards cutting taxes so that people have more money to exercise their choice, whether it be spoons, forks, knives or anything else.

Has anything amusing ever happened to you in connection with a spoon?

That's a marvellous question, and I firmly believe that the answer is no.

NEXT WEEK: Peter Jay – "Me and My Jay".

17

THOSE WORLD CUP RUGBY PIECES – A Private Eye Digest

by **Phil Space**

JONNY Wilkinson… blood, sweat and tears… fairytale ending… pride and glory… Jonny Wilkinson… sporting heroes… game for gentlemen… not like oiks in football… Jonny Wilkinson… not since 1966… national celebration… grown men crying… pubs full at breakfast… streets empty… Jonny Wilkinson… celebrations long into the night… return of masculinity… women as keen as men… Jonny Wilkinson… er… will this do? P.S.

The Daily Telegraph

The Golden Boot

England's Day Of Glory

AS A nation we are perhaps over-acquainted with bad news and with failure in the great international arenas. But now all that is in the past. With one glorious kick Conrad Black has been booted out of the boardroom and millions of Englishmen can now hold their heads up high once again.

Let us all celebrate the great victory over *(You're fired. M. Newboy, Ed.)*

NEW ZETA JONES THREAT

I'll sue anyone who says I'm litigious

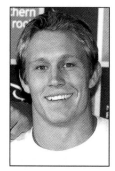

SHE DECIDED TO LIE BACK AND THINK OF ENGLAND

That Interview With Jonny Wilkinson In Full *(exclusive to the BBC and all newspapers)*

Interviewer: Jonny, what were your feelings as you watched the video of you kicking the goal that won the World Cup?

Wilkinson: It was a team effort.

I-SPY

WARNING UNCONTROLLED PEDESTRIAN CROSSING AHEAD

South London

Diversion →

Blackheath

CROMER IN BLOOM

Norfolk

HOTEL POSH

Odawara, Japan

CABBAGES & CONDOMS RESTAURANT
อาหารไทย ซี แอนด์ ซี สาขานครราชสีมา

Khorat, Thailand

Permissive bridleway

Hertfordshire

五 福
Gofuku

Japan

THREE BELL'S RESTAURANT CAFE&BAR

Side, Turkey

DMT MOBILE TOILET
ABUJA: 09-290-0501, 670-2557
LAGOS: 01-471-6578, 290-2924
"Shit Business is serious Business"
Otunba Gadaffi

Abuja, Nigeria

LAVANDERIA
irony and wash

Bari, Italy

Always Cutting Prices
~~£799~~
Only
£ 899

Currys, Brentford

↑ wee garden
← toilets

Isle of Bute

HUTTON
We apologise for any inconvenience caused by this work

Central London

HOTEL GREIF
⬆ 500 m

Innsbruck, Austria

A Taste of Olde England
THAI MENU • CARVERY • A LA CARTE • REAL ALE

Delivery van, Totnes

FREEMASONS RD E.16

Sunshine and smiles: Police share a joke at Europe's largest arms fair, in the Docklands, which opened to mainly peaceful protests

Metro

RESTAURANT ENNAAMA

Agadir, Morocco

STAYING PUT

staying put 🐕
WE ARE MOVING

Bexleyheath, Kent

RESTORAN FATSO
夜来香酒家

Malacca, Malaysia

BAR ANUS PUB

Puerto de la Cruz

SECONDHAND SHOP
AA driving school
0800 60 70 80

Canvey Island

Three steps to heaven.
whiskas whiskas whiskas

Richmond-upon-Thames

ATTENTION
Beach of irregular bottoms

Spain

Split 8 →
← Hotel Lav

Croatia

⬆ **VINTAGE SHEEP SHOW JUMPING LORRIES**

Okehampton

Toads in road

Isle of Wight

That Bush Visit Souvenir

I inherited this job from my father

Funny you should say that...

BAGHDAD TIMES

— FRIDAY NOVEMBER 28 2003 —
100 Dollars (or 2 cigarettes)

That Blair/Bush State Banquet Menu in full

Brown Nose Windsor Soup

— ✳ —

Grovellax

— ✳ —

Iraq Of Lamb with Crispy Fried Poodles and Condoleezza Rice

— ✳ —

Toady-in-the-Hole

— ✳ —

Suckling Up To Bush Pig

— ✳ —

From Off The Trolley

Bored Queen Of Puddings

— ✳ —

Nigelly and Custard

— ✳ —

Death by Choc 'n' Awe

— ✳ —

Coffee will not be served in case the Prime Minister suffers from a Cardiac Arrest

THOUSANDS OF US TROOPS STORM CAPITAL AND SEIZE PALACE

by Our Man In London
Comical Tariq Ali

The ancient city of London has never known anything like it.

Last night I watched with my own eyes as wave after wave of heavily armed US security personnel took over the capital with scarcely a shot being fired.

The streets were deserted as millions of inhabitants stayed at home to watch the rugby.

President Bush himself led the attack, first seizing the airport and then targeting the Palace, where Britain's religious leader Elizabeth II cowered in a cellar, terrified of being bored to death.

US propaganda chiefs had earlier predicted that the huge display of American firepower would be met by cheering crowds, grateful to the President for defending them against the weapons of mass destruction.

The Queen Mother Of Battles

But Londoners I spoke to were deeply resentful of the US invasion.

Said one, holding a 'Stop The War Banner', "We are fed up with the imperialist aggressor Bush and the puppet regime of his poodle Blair.

"We want to live in a country where the views of ordinary Londoners are *(cont'd. p. 94)*

Lowry's 'The Mill Owner Who Stole The Workers' Pension Fund' captures the spirit of the industrial North

When's happy hour?

As soon as you go home

20

Where They Stood On The Bush Visit

Harold Pinter, playwright

(Pause) I'd like to stand on Bush's head and kick his brains out. Not that he's got any. The bastard.

Andrew Motion, Poet Laureate

A small boy lies in the hospital
Without any arms
A poet sits at his desk
Without any ideas

(Will this do? A.M.)

Mark Steyn, columnist on the Bush Telegraph

The British should be out on the streets cheering. If it wasn't for the United States, the whole lot of you would have been speaking German and goose-stepping around like John Cleese. You're gutless and weak, all of you. No wonder you need Bush to save you! God Bless America!

Mayor Livingstone

George Bush is the biggest threat to planet earth since Darth Vader. If he had his way, he would kill all of us as if we were pigeons in Trafalgar Square. I urge all British newts to stand up and be counted.

Lord Really-Smugg

I well remember the visit of Woodrow Wilson in 1918, when he was kind enough to have lunch with me at the Garrick. I cannot disclose what we discussed, but it would certainly make some of today's protestors look rather foolish.

Dave Spart (leader of the Neasden Stop The Iraq War, Troops Out, Anti-Globalisation, Ban Killer GMOs, Free Nepal Rainbow Alliance)

Er, basically, sickening, oil, er, neo-con imperialism, Fascist Bush, er, traitor Blair, er, that's it.

STAFF SUPPORT CHARLES

I'm behind you, Sir

Not too close

NEWT MAN WREAKS HAVOC ON LONDON TRAFFIC AT COST OF BILLIONS

By Our Transport Staff
Jams Naughtie

A 57-YEAR-OLD single-parent father, dressed as a newt, today climbed to the top of London's City Hall to make a series of ridiculous demands.

The entire population of London will have to pay a huge price for the chaos inflicted on the capital by the stunt that went too far. "When he first got up there," said one cab driver, "we all thought it was a bit of a laugh. But now we've seen the effect of it all, I am beginning to think that stringing up would be too *(cont'd p. 94)*

(cont'd p. 94)

■ **CHARLES** – leave him alone for gawd's sake. The poor old Prince is only trying to do his best and what's his reward!!?!? To be pilloried in the press by every pea-brained palace pooftah with an axe to grind??!? Give him a break Mr Pressman and concentrate on the real news for a change – ie, Are Becks And Posh Washed Up??!!

■ **ARE BECKS AND POSH** washed up??!?!?! Who cares??!!!! When there are more burning issues to cover, like 'Is Chazza A Right Royal Shirtlifter'??!??!! Come on, Mr Pressman, we have a right to know and don't spare our blushes??!!!! It's high time this pampered prince was revealed in his true colours, ie pink!!! Geddit??!?!?! Prince of Wales??!?!! More like the Ponce of Wales!??!? No offence, Your Royal Highness, and after all you do work tirelessly for charity and cannot answer back!!?! Hats off to you!!?!

■ *DIANE ABBOTT – the Hackney Hypocrite!!!?! Telling us all to send our toddlers to the local sink school whilst she's shelling out taxpayers' money to buy a better deal for her little brat!!?!?! Do the decent thing, Diane, and shoot yourself!!?!?!* '

■ **THREE CHEERS** for Diane Abbott?!?! At last, there's one New

Labour mum who's not afraid to put her kiddie above her principles!!?!? Who wouldn't do the same if they were in her shoes??!?! Every mum wants the best for her little 'un and anyone who says different is a hypocrite!!?!?!?

■ **AAAH!!! BLESS??!?!** Didn't you have a little weep when you saw Macca, Heather and her little bundle of money??!?!!!? *(Surely 'joy'? Ed.)*

■ *READ IDS's new novel??!?!? It makes Jeffrey Archer look like Charles Dickens!!?!?! And that's saying something!!?? Glenda's rating: z-z-z-z-z-z.*

■ **HERE THEY ARE** – Glenda's Poppy Idols (Geddit!!?!?!?)

● **Bishop Gene Robinson** – You weren't always gay, were you??!? So why not let Aunty Glenda put you back on the straight and narrow!???! Geddit???!??!

● **Maurice Saatchi** – You're the new Chairman of the Conservative Party!???!? Pop round to my place, Mr Ad Man, and I can say "I 'ad you"!??! Geddit????!?

● **Sir Ranulph Twistleton Wickham Fiennes** – Crazy name, crazy marathon-running guy!!!

Byeeee!!!

DAILY Mirror

Friday November 28 2003

MIRROR IMPOSTOR SENSATION

by Mirrorman **PIERS MORON**

IT SEEMS scarcely possible that someone like me can just walk in off the street and become editor of the Daily Mirror, with no questions asked!

Yet that is the incredible truth behind what they are calling the security scandal of the Millennium!

I had no qualifications for the job. When I was asked for a reference, I arranged for one of my mates in the pub to vouch for me down the phone.

As for my dodgy past, no one seemed to give it a second thought.

Within a day I was given the freedom of the paper's palatial headquarters, and I was allowed to go anywhere and do whatever I liked.

FOOT-IN-MOUTH-MAN

It was amazing. If I had wanted to, I could have made the paper look silly by adopting completely contradictory editorial standpoints every couple of weeks.

I could have gone on television to make important

programmes about the evils of newspapers printing nothing but rubbish about celebrities.

I could even have put a reporter into Buckingham Palace and pretended I was doing it as a matter of national security.

But, almost unbelievably, I was able to sit in the top seat without being rumbled for seven years.

What was astonishing was that not once did anyone even challenge whether I should be there.

THE WORLD OF THE ARTS

Brian R Sewell reviews an exhibition of the Queen's furniture in the pages of the Daily Mirror

Eugh! One is instantly reminded of some dingy provincial hotel in Wolverhampton. One can almost taste the soggy Sunblest toast and the tiresome little plastic containers of that dubious substance which passes itself off as butter. And the very idea of dressing the

table with that hideous bouquet of no-doubt plastic flowers, more suited to Golders Green crematorium than a respectable breakfast table. And, my dear, who eats breakfast with one of those vulgar little transistor wireless sets next to the coffee pot, no doubt permanently tuned to the inanities of Classic FM, with its steady drip of popular melodies. And that lamp! An ill-judged bargain purchased at some Sandringham

car boot sale, perhaps? What are we to make of this phantasmagoria of suburban bad taste, this themeless pot pourri of petit-bourgeois banality, with its dralon tablecloth, easy to wash rayon duvets and, above all, Horror of Horrors, can this be true, a cornflakes container constructed from, wait for it, TUPPERWARE! *(At this point the author was overcome by such a fit of snobbery that he fainted away).*

VALE FARM

PICK YOUR OWN HOUSE

KenPyne

MURDOCH SHOCK

We're going to turn the Times into a tabloid

I thought we did that years ago

At last, a good story in the Telegraph. I've been fired

GNOMEBY'S

Grand Auction Sale

(in connection with the winding-up of the Estate of Lord and Lady Black, due to impending litigation and possible imprisonment)

LOT ONE

Very Fine And Agreeable Old Newspaper (known as the *Daily Telegraph*), offering considerable scope for imaginative improvement by the right owner.

The lot includes ownership of:

1 Brand-new Editor, only slightly used.

1 Former Editor (1807 vintage), still in perfect working order, answers to name "Deedes".

Assorted Hacks, all well connected, many Old Etonians or Roman Catholics or both.

LOT TWO

Equally Fine And Agreeable Sunday Newspaper, with only two previous owners.

The lot includes:

1 Well-connected Editor, brother of famous TV chef plus wide selection of advertisements for Stannah stairlifts, walk-in baths and easy-to-use garden tools (no bending, no kneeling, no aching back!)

LOT THREE

Venerable Old Weekly Magazine, very stained with some spotting (the *Spectator*). Planning permission for demolition has been obtained. Offers ample scope for redevelopment as weekly news magazine, with interesting, well-written articles and amusing cartoons.

The lot also includes:

1 Celebrity Editor (as seen on TV).

1 Very Soiled Greek Drug Addict (past sell-by date).

Sale by auction to start immediately

Nursery Rhymes Revisited

No. 94

Ba-ba-Barbara Black
Have you any money?
No sir, no sir,
The Hollinger shareholders
    have taken it all away.

(Anon)

What You Will See If Dirty Desmond Takes Over The Daily Telegraph

𝔇𝔞𝔦𝔩𝔶 𝔓𝔬𝔯𝔫𝔬𝔤𝔯𝔞𝔭𝔥

● **LIZ HURLEY** starkers **1**

● **JANET DALEY** answers your sex problems **5**

● **W.F. DEEDES** on sex in your Nineties **6**

● **READERS' WIVES** (formerly 'Letters From Tunbridge Wells') **7**

● **ALEXANDER SHULMAN** – Why naked is the new look for this year **8**

● **SANDHEK SEVKU** reviews the new films, including *'Asian Babes – The Movie'* and *'Big Ones Live'* **9**

● **COMMENT** – "Get 'em off, darling" says Christopher Howse **12**

● **IN THE CITY** – Neil Collins wants the Bonk Rate increased

PLUS our new pocket billiard cartoonist **SMUTT**

PLUS BORIS JOHNSON on his new-look magazine *'The Sextator'*!

SMUTT

Some of us want more Bush!!

Remember the slogan
'Read A Best-Selling Porn Mag Every Day'

POETRY CORNER

In Memoriam

So. Farewell
Then
Johnny Cash.

Famous country
Singer.

Yes, you were
Known as the
Man In Black.

Were I to
Attend your
Funeral,
I too would
Be the Man
In Black.

But Tennessee is
A long way
From Tooting.

And Ryan Air
Do not
Fly there.

E.J. Thribb (aged 17½)

PS: Apologies to
Leni Riefenstahl

For not writing a
Threnody,
Or a Thribbody
As they are known,
On the occasion
Of her death.

"The Woman In Black
Shirt".

Yes, that would have
Been a good title.

Or perhaps I
Should have used
It for Lady
Diana Mosley.

PPS: So Farewell
Then also David
Seaman.

You have
Retired from
Premiership
Football. You
Did not have
A catchphrase.

But then,
As Keith says,
In recent times,
'Catching' was not
Exactly your
Thing.

E.J.T

IT'S GRIM UP NORTH LONDON — KNIFE & PACKER

IT'S GRIM UP NORTH LONDON — KNIFE & PACKER

POETRY CORNER

In Memoriam Keiko the Whale

So. Farewell
Then Keiko –
Star of the film
Free Willy
And also
Free Willy 2.

Now, my friend
Keith says
You are
Really free
At last.

Which is
Quite poetic when
You think that
He is not a real
Poet.
Just a student
Reading media
Studies at the
University of
Wales.

A curious
Coincidence.

E.J. Thribb (17½)

In Memoriam Fanny Blankers-Koen, Dutch Olympic Athlete

So. Farewell
Fanny Blankers-
Koen.

You won four gold
Medals in 1948.

"The Flying
Housewife." Yes,
That was your
Nickname.

You were best
Known for your
Modesty.

Which is why I
Have never
Heard of you.

Until today.

E.J. Thribb (runner-up 2004
Whitbread Poetry Award for
his collection *A Barrowful of
Dead Leaves*, The Horovitz
Press, £69.99)

CHRISTMAS TO BE CANCELLED

by Our Cultural Staff **Polly Tickly-Correct**

THE SECRETARY of State for Culture, Tessa Jowell, announced yesterday that Christmas will no longer be celebrated in Britain in order not to offend anyone from a different faith, culture, ethnic background or sexual orientation.

She said, "The idea of a national public festival based on a minority religion such as Christianity is deeply offensive to the millions of people who I haven't asked about this but who I am sure would really hate the whole Christian mumbo-jumbo as much as I do.

"People should choose which religious festival they want to have at Christmas and there are dozens of much better ones. There's Hanakah, Divali, Ramadan and shopping at Bluewater just to name a few and there's no reason why we should be shoving Christmas down people's throats at this time of year."

Late News
TESSA JOWELL TO CLOSE DOWN ART GALLERIES

"These buildings are full of pictures painted by dead, white males", she told reporters, "and a majority of them feature scenes of a Christian theme which is obviously deeply offensive to the vast minority of people in this country."

Even Later News
TESSA JOWELL TO ABOLISH HERSELF

"I am a disgrace," she said. "I am white, middle-class and deeply offensive to everybody."

"Is there a choice of superbugs?"

What you won't see
NEWSNIGHT

Kirsty Wark *(for it is she)*: As the row grows over the so-called Holyrood scandal, there are questions over the role of Kirsty Wark at the centre of it all. I am joined in the studio by myself. Kirsty, these are serious allegations...

Kirsty: I...

Kirsty: First you sit on the selection panel for choosing the architects for the new parliament building. Then the BBC commissions your private company to make a documentary about it. Then when the whole project turns into a hugely expensive shambles, you won't hand over the tapes to the official enquiry...

Kirsty: Can I just say that…

Kirsty: No, no let me finish. Furthermore when you are questioned by the barrister at the inquiry, you fail to mention that you were a bridesmaid at his wedding.

It all smells pretty fishy doesn't it?

Kirsty: Well, let me ask *you* a question, Kirsty. How come *you* are still presenting Newsnight for the BBC when they should be broadcasting an investigation into *you*.

Kirsty: That's all very well, Kirsty, but what I'd like to know is how come the costs of *your* licence-payer funded documentary have gone through the roof? There's hundreds of thousands of pounds adrift here, aren't there?

Kirsty: Are you accusing me of impropriety? That's a bit rich coming from you.

Kirsty: How dare you?

Kirsty: I'm not going to sit here and listen to this.

Kirsty: Me neither.

(Both storm out in huge huff complaining they have been treated as if they were guests on Newsnight).

'SPIGGY IS F****** W*****' CLAIMS FELLOW TURD

by Our Pop Music Staff **C.D. Rom** and **D.J. Taylor**

A HUGE storm erupted last night when the 83-year-old lead guitarist of the Turds, a popular singing group formed early in the last century, launched a vicious attack on the group's lead singer, Spiggy Topes, for accepting a knighthood.

Said the old gentleman from his 412-room retirement home in Weybridge, Surrey, "Spiggy is a total b****** to my mind, for grovelling to the Queen, the totem pole of the Establishment, which back in the Sixties tried to have us all put in the Tower just because we smoked a few joints in the privacy of our toilets and that."

Hard Day's Knighthood

The elderly rock star's ravaged face creased in anger as he snarled, "Spiggy and me go way back, with hits such as *'Love Is The Thing, Hate Isn't'* (of which I incidentally wrote both the music and the words) and to what's left of my mind, it is a total war crime for him to accept a seat in the House of Lords, which totally flies in the face of everything we stood for."

Sri Lanka

"I am writing a protest song entitled *'Spiggy Is A Right C***'* for my new Christmas solo album which I hope to have in the shops by 1999."

Sir Spigismond was unavailable for comment last night as he is watching cricket as a guest of the President of Sri Lanka.

Sir Spigismond is 95.

JAGGER AND SON

I'm 92

And I just look it

LETTERS TO THE EDITOR

(Who he? Ed.)

Popular First Names

From Henry Porter-Kabin

Sir, As is customary at this time of year, I have compiled from your birth announcements a list of the most popular names of 2003. They are as follows:

GIRLS	BOYS
1 Kylie	1 Jonny
2 Madonna	2 Wilkinson
3 J.K.	3 Martin Johnson
4 Barbara Amiel	4 Frodo
5 Catherine Zeta	5 Gandalf
6 Kirsty	6 Arnie
7 Rebekah	7 Ozzy
8 Chardonnay	8 Prince William
9 Nigella	9 Hoogstraten
10 Yasmin-Alibhai	10 Justice Popplewell

Yours faithfully,
HENRY PORTER-KABIN,
The Old Temporary Dwelling, The Cotswolds, Glos.

Daily Mail

Has Christmas Become Too Commercial?

asks Max Hastings

EVERY YEAR it gets worse. The blatant attempt by cynical money-grubbers to make a quick buck out of what should be a religious festival makes me furious.

This year I noticed a particularly obvious attempt to cash in by a columnist writing in the Mail who could scarcely be bothered to conceal the fact that his only interest in Christmas was whether he could make £2,000 by writing a lazy why-oh-why piece about how commercial the *(cont. p. 94)*

Tomorrow: *Max Hastings asks "How bleeding is the obvious?"*

Very courageous decision.

That Grail business was a fiasco.

BIRCH

LANCELOT RETURNS HIS KNIGHTHOOD

IT wasn't exactly a surprise when the letter arrived offering me the chance to become a Member of the British Empire. After all, given the readership of this column, I am well aware that both the government and the monarchy want Polly "on side".

But what was the honour for? Was it on behalf of all working women juggling family and career, wiping the snotty noses of our infants whilst painting a Warhammer Orc Army and organising a dinner party for twenty, whilst simultaenously penning the best-selling *'Mummy For Old Rope'* (£7.99 and making a welcome reappearance in the Top Ten Books By Women Columnists Charts, *Sunday Times* 12.12.2003)??

Or was I being singled out because I have changed the way women think about themselves and their useless partners? We all have them, even Her Majesty, though I don't suppose Prince Philip spends Christmas slumped in front of *Pro-Celebrity Turkey-Strangling* presented by Clarissa Dickson-Wright and Hugh Fearnley-Whittingstall on Digital E47!!!

But after much soul-searching and in spite of everyone willing me to accept the honour – I just had to decline. And the reason was very simple. By refusing an MBE I've got in the papers again and it has even given me a subject for a whole column at a particularly desperate time of year! Happy New Year.
© *Polly Filler MBE.*

POETRY CORNER

Lines Written On The Decision By Miss Yasmin Alibhai-Brown To Return Her MBE To Her Majesty The Queen In Support Of The Similar Decision By The Universally-Acclaimed Ethnic Poet Mr Benjamin Zephaniah In Protest At The Shameful Record of British Imperialism Through The Past Twenty-Five Centuries

BY WILLIAM
REES-MCGONAGALL

'Twas in the year two-thousand-and-three

(Owing to the length of the title of this poem, the rest of the poem has had to be held over to a future issue)

THE MAKE UP OF THE NEW NORTHERN IRELAND ASSEMBLY

D.U.P	30 seats
Ulster Unionists	27 seats
Sinn Fein	24 tonnes of semtex, five hundred rocket-powered grenade launchers, seven hundred Kalashnikov sub-machine guns and three thousand petrol bombs *(surely "seats"? Ed)*.
S.D.L.P.	18 seats

MASS HONOURS FOR RUGBY

by Our New Year's Eve Staff **Holly Day Relief**

THE ENTIRE crowd of 750,000 supporters who turned out to salute the England rugby team in central London have been awarded the MBE in the New Year's Honours list as a recognition of their part in the World Cup victory.

"It is only fitting that the role of the fans should be recognised," said a government spokesman. "Many of them had to bunk off work or play truant from school and that kind of commitment should be rewarded by the nation."

When asked if this was just a desperate attempt to get 750,000 votes, the spokesman said, "Would you like to be Dame Holly of Day-Relief?"

LATE NEWS

THE rugby ball that Jonny Wilkinson kicked to win the Rugby World Cup for England is to receive a knighthood from the Queen.

A spokesman for the ball said, "The ball is absolutely over the posts at the news."

RESERVOIR NOBS

Let's go to church

Farewell to 'The Office'

by Our TV Staff **David Brent-East**

ONE OF Britain's best-loved comic characters finally bowed out over Christmas, after a two-year run, during which his absurd and embarrassing management style had rocketed him to the bottom of the polls.

The series starred Iain Duncan Cough as the gaffe-prone boss of Tory Central Office, whose attempts to inspire his down-trodden subordinates invariably ended in ignominious failure.

Viewers came to know some of the Offices's more improbable characters, such as Cough's dim-witted No. 2, Mike Ancram, the office prankster Ollie Letwin and the scarcely articulate receptionist Theresa May, constantly obsessed with her new shoes.

But the star of the show was unquestionably Cough himself, whose ability to get the wrong end of every stick and to say the wrong thing made him a national laughing stock, with a huge following (Sid and Boris Johnson).

The climax of the series came earlier last year when Cough's behaviour became so impossible that he had to be fired, and replaced by a smarmy colleague.

In the special Christmas edition viewers saw the redundant Cough embarrassing himself and everyone else even further by turning up to the office party, only for his former colleagues to ignore him.

THIS WEEK

LYNNE TRUSS

May I...

This column should strictly be called 'My Spoon And I'. This is a common error, but it is still an irritating one and I feel that such sloppiness should no longer be tolerated.

Has anything amusing ever happened to you in connection with a spoon?

I am not sure that one is connected "with" a spoon. This may be common usage nowadays, but there is a good case for the more traditional "connected to" or even the...

Thank you.

Lynn Truss is the author of the best-selling guide to punctuation and grammar 'Eats Spoons And Leaves'

The Interview You Won't Hear

Radio 4: The Today Programme

Humphrys: John Humphrys, surely you're paid enough by the BBC as it is? Why do you have to write that stuff in the Sunday Times?

Humphrys: I think I have as much right as anyone else to express my opinions in the press…

Humphrys: But that's not what I asked. And why should the BBC now compensate you for writing columns when you're meant to be working for them anyway?

Humphrys: I haven't got time to answer these questions...

Humphrys: No, let me finish...

Humphrys: No, let me finish.

Humphrys: I'm not standing for this.

Humphrys: Nor am I.

(Both storm off in a huff, protesting that they have been treated like guests on the Today programme.)

When I was your age, I used to steal apples

What are apples?

McLACHLAN

SOHAM

HUGE REALLY UNPLEASANT HEADLINE – GRUESOME DETAILS BELOW

By Our Court Staff **Pru Rient** and **Sandy Ghoul**

A COURT yesterday heard more really nauseating details about a disgusting murder.

No words can possibly do justice to just how revolting yesterday's proceedings were.

Shocking

Which is why we have devoted the whole of our front page, and half of today's paper, to spelling out in detail the full horror of what our entire news team has been able to report from the courtroom.

In addition we are able to cover several pages with pictures so moving that we hope they will help to sell lots of newspapers.

You might think that only the jury would need to know what exactly is happening in this horrifying case, and that the rest of the population could be kept quite adequately informed by means of a short court report on page 8, under the headline "Soham Case – Day 94". But no, we *(cont. p 2-24)*.

WHEN WILL THIS MEDIA CIRCUS END? by **Our Entire Staff**

THIS one-time sleepy Cambridgeshire village has become the unwelcome focus of a relentless media frenzy for over a year. The people of Soham are battered and bewildered and their one wish is to move on and be allowed to get on with their lives.

We spoke to over a hundred typical villagers through the letter-box, asking them "Do you want to move on and be allowed to get on with your lives?".

The answer was unequivocal – "Go away". And that is the message for the media. It is time to go away and then come back again for the first anniversary when we can run a supplement and *(cont. p. 94)*

IN THE SCOTTISH COURTS

McFayed v. Regina Day 94

Before Mr Justice Cocklecarrot

(The judge asked the McFayed of McFayed to state his case.)

McFayed: I am the McFayed of McFayed, Chief of the Ancient Clan of the McFayeds, known as the Fighting Fuggers of That Fuggin' Ilk.

Judge: Even in that kilt you do look a bit foreign to me. You have the look of a postcard salesman in Port Said. No offence.

McFugger: That is a fuggin' slur on the glorious name of the McFayeds and this orange and purple tartan bestowed on my clan after our glorious victory in the famous Battle of Harrods in 1983, when I slew the infamous 'Tiny' Rowland, known as 'Faintheart', with my bare hands.

Judge: Be that as it may, Mr McFayed, it says here in Bundle 94, and I quote, "the fuggin' Duke of Edinburgh killed Lady fuggin' Diana and should be fuggin' strung up, och aye the fuggin' noo".

McFayed: I am just claiming my basic human rights under Scottish law, as the Laird of Glen Fugg and the Master of Auld Crookie, to see justice done and to see the Duke and his wife swinging from the highest gibbet in the land, just like our Scottish heroes of old, William Wallace, William Connolly, Sean Connery and Robert the Fuggin' Bruce.

Judge: Quite so, Mr McFayed, but have you any evidence to support your case?

McFayed: Indeedy I fuggin' dody, Your Honour. The evidence is to be found in this brown tartan envelope which Your Lordship may find conclusive.

Judge: I think I need to retire and count up the evidence.

The case continues...

Tomorrow: In The Divorce Courts Justice Popplecarrot: *Legover Magnatum alleged with senior colleague's wife.*

Ground-breaking Ideas No 0001

Daily Mail

FRIDAY, DECEMBER 26, 2003

SADDAM CAPTURED — HOUSE PRICES TO RISE

by Our Political Staff
Joyce Rejoyce

THE DISCOVERY of the former President of Iraq, Saddam Hussein, in a hole near Tikrit has enormous repercussions for British and American policy in the Middle East, but it is even more significant for those in Middle England.

The beleaguered home owners of Britain have at last got a reason

Crowds cheering the news that the property market is buoyant again

to cheer, as the capture of the ex-dictator means increased confidence in the American economy, which will inevitably filter through to British interest rates, which will *(cont'd p. 94)*

IRAQIS CELEBRATE CAPTURE OF SADDAM

by Our Man In Baghdad **Rageh Omaar Sharif**

THOUSANDS of jubilant Iraqis took to the streets last night to celebrate the final humiliation of their former dictator by blowing themselves up and killing anyone within range. *(Reuters)*

LATE NEWS
IRAQ

PRESIDENT BUSH has warned that the capture of Saddam Hussein will not mean an end to violence in the region by fanatics.

"Donnie Rumsfeld tells me we've still got Iran and Syria to invade in 2005," said a jubilant President... *(cont. p. 94)*

SADDAM HUSSEIN has sent a defiant message to his supporters from his prison cell, urging them to "cower and hide from the American infidels to the bitter end".

"Allah expects each and every one of you to gloriously hide in a hole in the ground, petrified for your life in the face of the invaders," said the former Iraqi... *(cont. p. 94)*

PRESIDENT BUSH has mocked Saddam Hussein after his final

hiding place was revealed, saying "When the going got tough, you went and hid in a hole.

"This contrasts so starkly with my decision during 9/11 to secrete myself away in a proper underground bunker until all threat of danger had passed," said a jubilant... *(cont. p. 94)*

SADDAM'S TRIAL

I'm asking George Galloway to be a character witness

THAT SADDAM CAPTURE COVERAGE ON BBC NEWS 24 IN FULL

(9.32 am: Graphic filling half the screen flashes up – 'Breaking News – Saddam Captured')

9.34 am

Newsreader: ... breaking news just in, we're getting reports that Saddam Hussein has been captured in Tikrit. To discuss this, I'm joined now by the only defence analyst who was awake at this time on a Sunday morning. Rupert Hanwell, what would this arrest mean?

Hanwell: This would almost certainly mean that Saddam has been captured, unless he hasn't been, in which case this would mean that he hasn't.

Newsreader: Would you say it's significant that our breaking news banner that fills the bottom half of the screen is now twice as big and bright as Sky News?

Hanwell: Almost certainly.

10.02 am

Newsreader: We can cross now live to Baghdad to a reporter wearing a flak jacket with a microphone in their hand. John, what can you tell us?

Correspondent: We are getting reports here that Saddam Hussein has been captured.

Newsreader: And where are those reports coming from?

Correspondent: From people watching BBC News 24 from London via satellite.

10.48 am

Newsreader: We can cross now live to an empty room in Downing Street where we'll point the camera at a door for twenty minutes and speculate as to who might be standing beside it.

11.25 am

Newsreader: What effect will Saddam's capture have on the world of fashion? We're joined now by leading British designer Stella McCartney...
(Cont. for 94 hours)

The Sunday Telegraph

DECEMBER 21 2003

Is This Lord Lucan?

BY DOMINIC LAWSON

TODAY the Sunday Telegraph can exclusively reveal that the bearded man arrested in Iraq last night is none other than the missing peer Lord Lucan.

Shergar

The man, going under the assumed name of Saddam Hussein, has been in hiding for over 25 years after the murder of his nanny, living quietly as the President of Iraq.

Now, thanks to an investigation by top Sunday Telegraph reporters, the world can know the truth. 'Jungly Saddam' is none other than

SADDAM HUSAYN AL-TIKRITI
President

Lucky Lucan. His winning streak has finally *(cont. p. 94)*

ON OTHER PAGES ● Will Saddam bid for ailing Telegraph? **7**
● Where is other missing peer, Lord Black? **10**

GNOMEBY'S

OF BAGHDAD (Est. 2003)

(Bomb Crater Street, next to burned-out tank)

Important Sale of Memorabilia

(formerly the property of an Iraqi gentleman)

Lot One

1 taxi (licence no. Tikrit 1), some bullet holes in bodywork and windscreen, but otherwise in good condition.

Lot Two

1 pistol, unused, bearing inscription 'The Lion Of The Euphrates Will Not Die Without Taking A Million Infidels With Him'. Accompanied by sales receipt from the Matrix Churchill Supergun Co, Coventry, counter-signed by the Rt. Hon. Alan Clark MP.

Lot Three

1 cabin trunk, enamelled with initials 'S.H.' and the insignia of the Army and Navy Stores, London SW1, containing $750,000 in mint dollar bills, formerly the property of other deceased persons.

Lot Four

1 torch.

Lot Five

I blanket in need of cleaning.

Lot Six

1 beard (false).

Guide price for all items: 4p

Gnomeby's – "We're On The Sunni Side Of The Street!"

NEW WAITING LIST SHOCK

by Our Medical Staff **Sue Perbug**

THE NHS was in crisis again last night when new figures were released showing that in the majority of British hospitals some bacteria had to wait "up to three days" to be admitted.

Said one furious lethal germ, "It's a disgrace. I had to wait for ages. There was literally no place for me to go. All the hospitals were choc-a-bloc with bugs. Finally, someone failed to wash their hands and I got into an old people's ward."

He continued, "I had considered going private but, frankly, bugs like me just can't get into those hospitals at all."

Venus de J-Lo

Notes & Queries

QUESTION: What is the origin of the Portakabin?

☐ REVEREND C.J. Barkworth is wrong in insisting that the word comes from the noted Alsace wine *Porto Cabino*, a favourite with English sailors who had visited Geneva, and which they drank in the cramped conditions of their wooden ships. The truth is more mundane, I'm afraid, in that the Portakabin originated in the French court of King Louis XIV ('The Sun King') who, when nature called, would cry out to his attendants "Portez le cabinet". The court dignitaries would then have to watch Louis performing his toilette. Later, to preserve the King's dignity, a small wooden shelter was assembled around the monarch and this gave rise to the abbreviated 'Portakabin' that we know today. Readers may be interested to note that there is a surviving example in *La Musée de la Toilette* in Limoges dating from 1608 (approx). *Professor Terry Duckfield.*

Question: Who was the first person to swim the Atlantic?

☐ INTERESTINGLY, it was a woman, Mrs Bridget O'Cohen, who, on 17th August 1872, set off from the tiny fishing village of Port O'Kabin in Co. Galloway and collapsed on the beach of the Massachusetts resort of Cape Dworkin, an epic 18 years, 216 days and three hours later. On her arrival, the unemployed Irish laundress confessed that she had intended to swim to Liverpool to visit her married sister, who had sadly died in the intervening years. Heartbroken at the news, she immediately turned round and swam back to Ireland, breaking her own record by six years. *Sister Ludmilla O'Cohen (great grand-daughter), The Dunswimmin Priory, Solihull.*

"We can't agree on 'Love Actually'"

STRING UP THIS DOG!

The face of evil

Say Simon Heffer and Peter Hitchens
The Columnists You Can't Read

THE NATION has been shocked by the savage murder of a defenceless corgi by a ruthless bull terrier. No one is in any doubt as to the identity of this psychopathic serial killer.

Yet the do-gooders, the Guardian-readers and animal rights brigade are quick to tell us that Princess Anne's favourite dog is in need of help rather than the rope.

What utter nonsense! If these lettuce-eating weirdos had their way (assisted no doubt by the Archbishop of Canterbury and his gay friends), the only punishment for this murderer would be to be put up at the taxpayer's expense in luxury kennels for the rest of it's life, and be fed round-the-clock Winalot in between sessions with the kennel therapist.

And even then the killer pooch would be back on the streets in 18 months, and ready to kill again!

No! There is only one answer to this menace. Princess Anne's mad dog should be strung up at once, for it is the only language that such a killer canine can understand.

Bringing back the rope would send a long overdue message to every murdering mongrel in Britain.

Just imagine a land in which Rover, Patch and Fido can once again walk safely down the streets, without Her Royal Highness's psychotic pooch burying it's teeth in their necks just for the fun of it!

© Dacretrash Productions 2004

THE FATKINS DIET
A Correction

IN RECENT WEEKS, we may have inadvertently given our readers the impression that the Fatkins Diet, which involves eating huge amounts of fried bacon, eggs, sausages and steak, was the basis of a healthy regime that would encourage weight loss.

This was due to a typographical error in which the words "huge amounts of fried bacon, egg, sausage and steak" mistakenly appeared in place of the words "fresh fruit, green vegetables and plenty of exercise".

We apologise to all those readers who have died of coronary disease as a result of following the Fatkins diet.

"Does my bum look big out of this?"

GADDAFI PROMISES TO DESTROY 'WEAPONS OF NON-EXISTENCE'

by Our Political Staff **W.M. Deedes**

COLONEL GADDAFI, the Libyan leader, has announced that, as of today, he is going to get rid of all the weapons that he does not possess and cease manufacture of any more weapons of the type that he hasn't been making.

His decision was greeted as a breakthrough by western leaders. The British Prime Minister, in a specially convened television broadcast, told the nation, "This is an extraordinarily brave decision by Colonel Gaddafi and I salute his courage. For an Arab leader to volunteer to give up his Weapons of Non-Existence (WNE) sends a strong signal to the rest of the Middle East. And that message... *'the West will give you loads of money if you tell us what we want to hear'.*

THE SUN

Hands Off Rebekah's Boobs!

IF the Sun's editor wants to make a tit of herself attacking Clare Short then why should the killjoys stop her!

If she wants to make her newspaper look ugly and stupid then it is no business of anyone else!

If Rebekah wants to demonstrate that she's a prize arse then good luck to her!

After all, it's what the Sun is famous for! Rebekah's boobs are a fine British tradition that we should all be proud of and fight to keep!

Here's a picture of what Rebekah would look like if she were the same age as Clare Short and the Sun had stuck HER head on someone's body instead of Clare's!

Talk about a Bum idea to try and rescue falling sales figures! It's the bottom of the barrel!

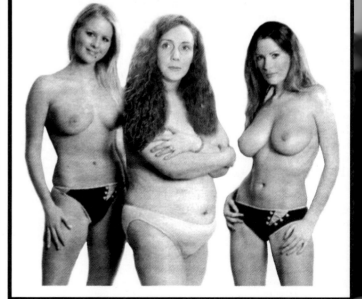

Curse of Gnome Strikes Down Lawyer

by Our Legal Staff **Joshua Rozenbeard**

THE legendary Curse of Gnome has struck again, I can reveal. This time the victim was the 89-year-old former solicitor, Peter Carter-Ruck, named in the Guinness Book Of Records as the world's richest libel lawyer.

Carter-Ruck, 102, had for years lived under the dreaded curse after his many legal actions against Private Eye magazine.

Yet, for all the precautions he took, the Curse caught up with him when he was struck down tragically early in his 107th year by a fatal attack of old age.

(Reuters)

Dear Sir,

Our attention has been drawn to the above article in which our client, myself, has been portrayed as a grasping and avaricious man whose sole motivation was the acquisition of huge quantities of money. This is prima facie a gross libel, the gravity of which is only compounded by it being true.

However, due to the fact that I am dead, and therefore technically non in positione suerensis, *my client is prepared to dispose of the matter on the following conditions:*

1. An apology in open court in terms to be dictated by myself.

2. The payment of a token sum in lieu of damages (£10 million).

3. The settlement in full of all my legal costs, amounting, shall we say, to a modest £25 million.

Yours, The Late P. Carter-Ruck, Beelzebub & Co, Old Nick Street, Hades EC4

The Wit And Wisdom Of Britain's Greatest Stand-Up Lawyer

Q. Guess where I like to stay when I'm in London?
A. The Ritz! *(Writs)*

Q. What do you call a man who's sued Private Eye?
A. Rich! *(Wealthy)*

Q. What did the top libel lawyer call his daughter?
A. Sue! *(Legal term for issuing a writ)*

Q. What has Peter Carter-Ruck got in common with Tim Henman?
A. They've both made a lot of money in court! *(Tennis/Legal)*

Q. How many libel lawyers does it take to change a lightbulb?
A. Seventeen. One articled clerk to file request for lightbulb change (£50 an hour). Three para-legal secretaries to research lightbulb change procedures (£75 an hour). One approved competent person to inspect socket in accordance with Health & Safety Act 1974, as amended by EC Directive 90/270, as implemented by Changing of Lightbulbs in the Workplace Regulations 1994 (£150 an hour). Two junior partners to scrutinise above statutory instruments to ensure full compliance (£250 an hour). Two senior partners to review the firm's lightbulb policy over luncheon at the Garrick Club (£400 an hour). One finance director to receive submission of expenses claim from senior partners (£650 an hour). One Queen's Counsel to provide learned opinion on the arguments for and against the necessity of changing the bulb (£1000 an hour). One very senior partner (P. Carter-Ruck) to explain to client that due to circumstances beyond the firm's control it would be inadvisable to proceed with the matter of the lightbulb and that he had pleasure in enclosing his firm's charges (£50,000), which, under the terms of contract required immediate payment.

"Did I tell you that Granny has out-sourced her knitting to an Asian workshop?"

The Daily Brillograph

Friday, January 23, 2004

'Older Men Are More Sexy' – Official

BY W.F. DEEDES

Brillo: Come back to my pad

A SURVEY carried out by the Daily Brillograph has good news for Britain's middle-aged men.

Figures show that young, beautiful women much prefer the company of gentlemen in their fifties and above.

Said one twenty-something, oriental interviewee, "My ideal lover is about fifty-five, with a Scottish accent and a distinguished record in the media industry. He should wear a vest, a baseball cap and have hair like an old-fashioned pan scourer. Blokes like that are just yummy!"

Poll details in full **2, 3, 4**

Brillograph City News

Q: *Who are they, the mystery brothers who now own the Brillograph?*
A: *None of your business*

Gilbert and George Barclay, the shy duo

MATT

TELEGRAPH SOLD SHOCK

'What?! Wasn't it given away free on a train...?'

"I think I've already seen this training video"

SHIPMAN SPECIAL

as heard on all channels

Presenter: Your mother was killed by Dr Shipman. How did you feel when you heard the news of his suicide?

Interviewee: Well... I... er...

Presenter: Did you feel angry that he'd cheated justice...

Interviewee: ...er...

Presenter: ...or did you feel traumatised as all the memories of that awful time came back to you?

Interviewee: ...er... I...

Presenter: Did you feel like crying? Perhaps you'd like to cry now? After all, your mother was murdered in cold blood by this monster. Isn't that worth a few tears?

Interviewee: Well, it's just that...

Presenter: It would really help if you could cry now. 'T's and 'Er's are no good to me. There are a lot of people out there who are waiting for you to break down. I mean, this man killed your mother, your closest relative. What does it take to wring a few tears out of you? What is wrong with you? *(Continued for several hours on all media)*

A Cab Driver Writes

Every week a well-known taxi driver is invited to comment on an issue of topical importance.

THIS WEEK: **Dave Blunkett** (Cab No. 14325) on the suicide of Dr Harold Shipman.

Crack open the bubbly, eh, guv! What a bastard! Cheating justice, that's what I call it. How dare he top himself like that instead of doing his full time? What did he get for killing all those old ladies up in wherever it was? 258 years? Not long, if you ask me! And what a bloody waste of money that would have been, keeping him inside for all those years. Do you know what should have happened to him? He should have been strung up! It's the only way to deal with people like him. And there's a question I want answered, guv! What were all those warders doing? I mean, it was obvious he was going to bump himself off! Tell you what, there should be a full top-level inquiry. Still, what a waste of money that would be.

Why does everyone keep going on about it, anyway? He's dead, innee? And that's a result! Bastard!

Blimey! I've just driven into something, guv. Aargh!

Next week: Mel Phillips (Cab No. 73842) on "The Myth Of Global Warming".

THE Sun SAYS

BRITAIN once again leads the world!

We may no longer be able to produce a Wimbledon champion or a winning football team.

But, make no mistake, this country has at last produced a global superstar who has no equal!

Forget the German Cannibal! Forget the Washington Sniper! Forget even that Russian looney with the beard whose name we can't remember.

When it comes to serial killing, it's still a British lad who takes the gold!

Whatever his faults (and the Sun has been the first to say he wasn't perfect), Hyde GP, Harold Shipman, has put Britain at the top of the world!

The Devil will see you now, Dr. Shipman.

RECEPTION

BIRCH

THOMAS THE PRIVATISED TANK ENGINE

BY THE REV. TAWDRY

"I'VE had a brilliant idea," said the Fat Controller. "What's that?" said Thomas.

"I think that the trains and the track should be run by the same company. That way, it would have an interest in making sure both parts worked properly."

"That's the way we used to do it," sighed Thomas. "I've been telling you this for years."

"Oh dear," said the Fat Controller. "Even my ideas are late."

© The Rev. Tawdry Blair 2003.

This Year's Must-Have All-Action Toy!

BUSH LIGHTYEAR

SPACE RANGER

The cartoon character who is going to Mars and who thinks he's the President of the United States. Press his buttons and he will say one of his three famous phrases:

"Bush Lightyear to the rescue"

"I come in peace or rather I don't"

"To infinitude and Beyoncé"

Price: $700 billion

EVERYTHING GIVES YOU CANCER

U.S. SCIENTISTS have revealed the results of a shocking study that says that everything gives you cancer.

"We'd always assumed that everything gives you cancer," said the scientist leading the study, "but now we have proof that everything you've ever eaten, inhaled, sprayed upon yourself or even brushed up against gives you cancer.

"Our advice is for people to kill themselves now rather than risk doing anything, since that is almost certain to lead to death and *(cont. p. 94)*

"Sad? Not at all. I mean, anything that encourages them to read..."

(Shot of large agreeable castle Toad Hall, with notice reading "Weasels, Stoats And Wogs Keep Out!". Flashy open-topped sports car screams to halt on gravel as servants run for cover. Alan Toad MP [for it is he] takes off goggles and jumps out of car)

Voiceover *(reading from Toad Diaries)*: July 3 1987. In high spirits, after driving back from terrific lunch with Ratty at my club. We discussed what a shit Badger is. Got squiffy on three bottles of Kenneth Grahame's '61 port.

(We see Toad being welcomed at the door of Toad Hall by his loving rottweilers)

Toad: Hullo Hitler. Hullo Goebbels. Hullo Bruce Anderson. That darkie postman's coming up the drive. Go get him!

(Amusing shot of postman throwing letters in the air as he is pursued by slavering hounds)

Toad Voiceover: Went round to Daphne Dormouse's flat in Belgravia.

(Shot of Toad entering agreeable room, taking off trousers as he does so)

Toad: You're a cracking piece of tottie, Daffers, aren't you, and no mistake!

Daphne Dormouse: Oo, you are a one, Toady!

Toad: What time does your father, Judge Dormouse, get back home from Court?

Daphne: Don't worry, Toady, we've got at least an hour.

(Enter Judge's wife Lady Dormouse and a succession of his other daughters)

Toad: I say, the more the merrier! Poop, poop!

What You Won't See

THE TOAD DIARIES

as dramatised for BBC94

(Cut to scene in the Riverbank Club, Pall Mall, with chairs full of senile moles, rats, badgers and Sir Peregrine Worsthorne)

Badger: Toad, I have to tell you, you're getting a bit of a reputation, if you know what I mean. You've got to stop gallivanting about and cut down on the drinking. Your father, Lord Toad of Civilisation, would be ashamed of you!

(Portuguese waiter arrives with huge

---

brandy for Toad)

Toad: Thanks, dago chummie!

Badger: And you'll have to stop flogging muskets to those Iraqi stoats. It's against the law, you know. Take a leaf out of young Mole's book. He's a coming man and knows when to lie low.

Toad: That's because he's a bloody mole, you prig! I hate black-nosers like mole!

Voiceover: After seeing Badger, I realised that I'd blown it! What a fool I am! What a miserable toad I am. I will never be made Deputy Under-Secretary for Picnics and Road Safety unless I learn how to keep my trap shut. Must give up drink and women.

(Cut to shot of drunken Toad with blonde companion, Miss Daisy Rabbit, by his side, careering down country lane at 80 mph and over-turning car in ditch)

Toad: That's blown it! It'll all be in the News of The Wildwood tomorrow.

Next Week: Toad comes up before Mr Justice Dormouse on assorted traffic offences, including arms-dealing and adultery.

CAST IN FULL

MR TOAD	LESLIE PHILLIPS
BADGER	WILLIAM WHITELAW
DAPHNE DORMOUSE	EMILIA FOX
DAISY RABBIT	AMANDA HOLDEN
RATTY	JOHN MAJOR
MOLE	MICHAEL PORTILLO
OLD WASHERWOMAN	MRS THATCHER
FIRST WEASEL	SIR DAVID FROST

THE TIMES JANUARY 23 2004

LETTERS TO THE EDITOR

Sir, I hold no brief for Mr Kilroy-Silk, but he is quite wrong in claiming that the Arabs have made no contribution to civilisation. One has only to think of the great 8th Century astronomer Ibn Al Koren (765-883), who not only invented the bicycle, the coffee grinder and the electric toaster, but also came up with the theory of relativity a full 1600 years before Einstein.

Yours faithfully,
REV. SIMON FLOWERDEW,
The Old Cottage, Cleethorpes.

Sir, I have never watched Mr Kilroy-Silk's performances on television, nor have I ever read the Sunday Express. However, may I point out that, while we Europeans were languishing in the Dark Ages, the Arabs were inventing football, potato crisps and television, a fact ignored by Mr Kilroy-Soap in his ill-informed

rant in the Spectator.
Yours sincerely,
ARTHUR STOVEPIPE (Sir),
(former Ambassador to the Sultanate of Oman), Dorset.

Sir, Whilst I hold no brief for the Arabs, it must be admitted that they are a bunch of murderous towel-heads who, given the chance, would blow us all to smithereens in a couple of sheikhs!
MIKE GIGGLER,
Via email.

Sir, Whilst I absolutely deplore the odious and racist sentiments expressed by Mr Killjoy-Slick and wholly support the BBC's decision to suspend him, surely in a democracy we should all have the right to express our views freely, especially if the speaker believes that all Arabs are homicidal terrorists who are clearly strangers to the benefits of a deodorant.
Yours sincerely,
COLONEL TWISTON DAVIES,
The Old Telegraph, Canary Wharf.

Daily Mail

Have You Noticed That The Days Are Getting Longer?

asks Sir Max Hastings, Britain's Top Columnist

HAVE YOU noticed that, since Christmas, the days are getting longer? And that means more daylight for everyone!

Hasn't that got to be good news for all of us? Except of course for those oddballs and weirdos who actually like the dark.

Personally, I actually *(cont. p. 94)*

© *Hastingstrash Productions 2004.*

"For God's sake Acton, slow down. Speed camera!"

Daily Mail

FRIDAY, JANUARY 23, 2004

DID FALL IN HOUSE PRICES CAUSE DIANA'S DEATH?

by Our Entire Staff

SENSATIONAL new evidence from the Scotland Yard Inquiry into the death of Diana, Princess of Wales shows that there may have been a link between the 2% fall in house prices in 1997 and the fatal crash which *(cont. p. 94)*

ON OTHER PAGES
■ **Was Shipman Murdered By The Duke Of Edinburgh?**
asks Mohamed Fayed

NEW DIANA THEORY

by Our Royal Staff **James Jenny Bond**

AN INCREDIBLE new explanation for the death of the late Princess Diana has been offered to the British public in the last few days.

The extraordinary theory claims that the Princess was not, as everyone thought, murdered by the Duke of Edinburgh and MI6, but was instead killed in a car crash because the driver was drunk.

The theory goes even further with wild allegations that there was no big flash in the tunnel, no switching of blood samples and no secret service agents tampering with the car brakes.

However, a number of Dianologists were quick to pour scorn on the new non-conspiracy theory, "This is clearly the work of internet lunatics," said one, "who seek to find an absurd story to account for events which have a perfectly rational explanation – i.e. space aliens in league with the Duke of Kent and Dotty the Bull Terrier flew through a time-hole causing a *(cont. p. 94)*

TV Highlights

Timewatch (BBC2), 9.00pm

'Charles Was Not Mad,' Says George III

Despite the evidence that Prince Charles spoke to flowers, threw furniture at his wife and told his mistress that he wanted to be a tampon, King George III claims that his distant relative was as sane as he was. Speaking from the grave, the late King George III told an oak tree in Windsor Great Park, "Charles suffers from the delusion that he is going to be King, but apart from that he *(Cont. p. 94)*

The Daily Tudorgraph

Friday, January 23, 2004

HENRY V TO RESIGN FROM ARMY

by Our Defence Staff W.M. Deedes

THE HERO of Agincourt, King Henry V, has announced that he is going to quit the army and has admitted feeling "disillusioned" following the stunning victory over the French.

Falstaff Officer

Henry V is famous for his rousing speech on the eve of battle which won many admirers around the world and was even compared with speeches by the legendary British commander Colonel Tim Collins.

But now Henry is to turn his back on a military career that has seen him capture Harfleur, defeat the evil Dauphin and earn the fealty of the Dukes of Burgundy and Orleans.

Pistol Whipped

"Henry is fed up with army life," said his wife Katherine. "He was accused of war crimes, subjected to a questioning of his integrity and rubbished in the media by Shakespeare."

She added, "Henry couldn't stand the bureaucracy and the political correctness any longer. All that paperwork about the Salic Law drove him barmy."

Once More Unto The Breach Of The Health & Safety Act

Henry is also believed to have been furious about the equipment used on the battlefield. Friends say that there was a shortage of cavalry which led to an over-dependence on the ground-to-air longbows and some Welsh soldiers only had leeks with which to "beat about your pate upon St David's Day" and *(cont. Act V. Scene 94)*

"I think I'd rather look for another cashpoint"

HUTTON – THE HISTORIC VERDICT

Private Eye's 94-page Cut–Out–'n'–Keep Souvenir Supplement

KEY PLAYERS

"Good man, great war leader, totally innocent of any impropriety."

"Mentally unstable, knew he'd been caught out, understandably ended his own life."

"Man of un-impeachable integrity, complete devotion to truth."

"Loathsome reptile. If he had an ounce of integrity he would have followed Dr Kelly's example."

"Outstanding public servant, not responsible in any way for anything."

"Recklessly irresponsible, lowest form of gutter journalism, would do well to follow example shown by Dr Kelly."

NO WMD FOUND IN HUTTON REPORT

by Our Intelligence Staff **Conrad Blix**

AFTER an exhaustive search through the arid wastes of the Hutton report, inspectors hoping to find ammunition which would blow Tony Blair and his government away have been forced to abandon the search.

Thousands of hacks have combed through over 150,000 square miles of paper, only to conclude "There is not a single weapon of mass destruction to be found anywhere in the Hutton report. We have been badly let down by our intelligence – or rather Lord Hutton's lack of it.

"We were definitely led to believe that Hutton was a highly dangerous operator, who had the capacity to destroy Tony Blair within 45 minutes of his report being published.

"Yet, when we got in there and began our search, all we found was a huge pile of rusty old tins containing low-grade whitewash."

Public School News

Shrewsbury School Shamed By Judge – "Hutton has disgraced our school" says Old Boy.

Biased, inaccurate and irresponsible... but enough of my report

MILLIONS TO BE CHARGED WITH CONTEMPT OF COURT

by Our Legal Staff **Joshua Rosenbeard**

LORD Hutton is reported to be 'furious' at the way in which his report has been treated by large numbers of the public. He is minded to make a court ruling that all those millions of people who have expressed their contempt for his report by claiming that it is a feeble whitewash and an insult to the intelligence of the public should be sentenced to a term of imprisonment in Guantanamo Bay.   *Reuters*

MOON MADE FROM CHEESE

HUTTON'S SHOCK FINDING

Full story pages 2, 3, 4, 6, 7-24.

ELVIS ALIVE AND WORKING IN SUPERMARKET

Hutton Inquiry Latest

Full story pages 24-36.

Friday, February 6, 2004

'BBC GUILTY – WATCH SKY INSTEAD'
says Hutton

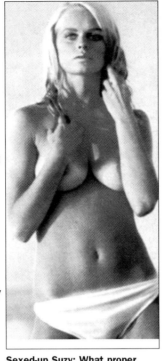

Sexed-up Suzy: What proper news journalism looks like!

By Our Entire Staff
REBEKAH DISH

THE distinguished judge, Lord Hutton, has concluded that the BBC should be closed down and all of its broadcasting responsibilities reassigned to Sky TV.

The judge blamed the BBC for irresponsible journalism, distortion of the facts and illegally diverting potential profits from shareholders of reputable satellite television companies into public service broadcasting which *(cont. p. 94)*

Late News

'KELLY DID NOT COMMIT SUICIDE'

AN AMAZING new claim by an expert witness last night cast doubts on the 'death by suicide' verdict on Dr David Kelly.

"It's quite obvious," said Mohamed Fayed, "that Dr Kelly was murdered by the Duke of Edinburgh assisted by MI6."

HUTTON: BBC Hits Back At Government

We surrender!

HUTTON CLEARS HITLER – 'Churchill And BBC To Blame'

by Our Inquiry Staff **Michael Whitewash**

'Evil man' – Hutton

IN A 2-million page report published today, the eminent High Court judge Lord Hutton absolved the late Adolf Hitler of "any blame whatever" for his part in the Second World War.

In his concluding remarks, Lord Hutton firmly pinned the blame on the former journalist Winston Churchill, whom he described as "a reckless, impulsive and irresponsible sensation-monger, who exaggerated the truth in order to further his own ambitions."

Lord Hutton reserved special blame for the British Broadcasting Corporation, which had given "an inordinate amount of air-time to broadcast his one-sided and ill-founded attacks on Herr Hitler, a man of unimpeachable integrity".

Hutton Dressed As Lies

It was in 1946 that Lord Hutton was asked by the government to carry out a thorough investigation into the circumstances surrounding the death of 60 million people during World War Two.

Lord Hutton heard evidence from several million witnesses, who told the judge that Hitler had taken over the Sudetenland and had then invaded Denmark, Norway, Belgium, France, Holland and a number of other countries.

Lord Hutton concluded that this could be interpreted as "a perfectly natural defensive reaction by the leader of the Third Reich in response to the threatening behaviour of Mr Churchill, whose one aim, it seemed, was to bring down the lawfully elected government of Herr Hitler and his colleagues".

Lord Hutton is 94 not out.

BBC News
(on all channels)

Newsreader: The Hutton Report has condemned the BBC for allowing Andrew Gilligan's unscripted 'two-way' report on the Today programe to be broadcast. I'm joined now by another BBC journalist who happened to be walking past the studio.
(Bemused-looking journalist is thrust into the seat opposite her)

Newsreader: So what's your reaction to the criticisms of the Corporation in the Hutton Report?

BBC Journalist: Well, I'd prefer to read the full report before making any snap...

Newsreader: Yes, but has the BBC learnt the lesson that you can't just let journalists on the air without tightly scripting what they're saying?

BBC Journalist: Probably. I mean, it's just my opinion, but I'm not sure...

Newsreader: So you don't think this sort of thing could happen again?

BBC Journalist: Look, I don't know, I was just on my way to make a cup of tea...

Newsreader: So, sum up the entire 328-page report in one sentence.

BBC Journalist: 'Rubbish from start to finish... BBC innocent of all charges...' oh, no, I bet I regret saying that... *(continued for 94 days)*

39

THE BBC
AN APOLOGY

IN RECENT years we may have given the impression that the British Broadcasting Corporation led by Greg Dyke was both hopelessly in decline and pathetically in thrall to the Labour Government.

Headlines such as 'Roland Rat Man Dumbs Down News', 'Tony's Croney Makes It "The Blair Broadcasting Corporation"' and 'Privatise The BBC Now' may have reinforced readers' perception that we believed the BBC to be failing the nation and that Mr Dyke was personally responsible for this failure.

We now realise that there is not a scintilla of truth in these allegations and that moreover the BBC is the jewel in the crown of British culture, particularly when led by such an inspiring figure of integrity as Sir Gregorian Dykeworth.

We apologise unreservedly to the Corporation and to Sir Gregorian for any confusion we may have caused by our coverage of the Corporation's affairs.

© Copyright all newspapers except the Times. See today's headline *'Why Rupert Murdoch should be the new Director General'*.

THE NEW POST-HUTTON BBC
HOW IT WILL LOOK

OUT GOES	IN COMES
The Today Programme	The Toady Programme
Ten O'Clock News	No. 10 News
Question Time	No Question Time
Panorama	Spinorama
Top Of The Pops	Top Of The Ups
University Challenge	University Fees
Newsnight With Jeremy Paxman	Newsnice With Jeremy Yesman
Just A Minute	Just 45 Minutes
PM	PM
24-Hour Rolling News	24-Hour Rolling Heads

(That's enough. Ed.)

BRITISH 'FBI' LAUNCHED

by Our Crime Reporter **Elliot Mess**

THE HOME Office today confirmed the establishment of the SOCA (The Serious Organised Crime Agency), touted to be the British equivalent of the FBI, at a cost of some eighty million pounds to the taxpayer.

"The activities investigated by the agency were previously carried out by an organisation known as the police," said a Home Office Minister, "however we felt that "police" wasn't a sexy enough name to get us lots of coverage in the newspapers, hence the creation of SOCA.

"We are confident that the Serious Organised Crime Agency will pay for itself as it generates unprecedented press coverage over the next twelve months, especially if it becomes the setting for a crime drama on ITV starring Robson Greene or Ken Stott."

That New Atheist Assembly In Full

Head: Our Father who doesn't exist.

All: Amen.

Head: We will now have a moment of reflection where we ponder on the fact that there is no God.

(Silence)

(There will then follow a reading from the works of a well-known atheist. It may be P.B. Shelley or it may be Sir Jonathan Miller)

Head: And now the creed.

All: We believe that you shouldn't believe in anything. Except the fact that there is nothing to believe in. Amen.

(There then follows a popular song. It could be 'My Old Man's An Atheist' or similar)

(That's enough Assembly. Ed.)

'Wise Men' Were Probably Women Priests, Says C of E

by Our Religious Affairs Staff **Christina O'Booze**

IN THE biggest shake-up the Church of England has known since last week, the Synod has ruled that the so-called "Three Wise Men" were not "wise" or "men", and were probably "only two in number".

"The most sensible explanation of this ridiculous old story," says top theologian Dr Agatha Nostick, "is that the Magi (from the Persian 'Maggi', a great female leader) were in fact a same-sex couple of high-ranking Chaldean princesses who were hoping to find a baby which social workers would allow them to adopt."

● Another long-overdue reform, proposed by the Synod, is that Church services should no longer be held on Sundays, but should be held at more suitable times, eg weekday evenings when there is no football on television.

SMOKING REALLY IS BAD FOR YOU

More shock revelations on other pages.

Pope revealed to be a Catholic **9**   Bears do defecate in woods **25**

"Amazing how many places have an integrated coffee shop these days"

That Terry Wogan Honorary Degree Citation In Full

SALUTAMUS TERENTIUM WOGANENSIS POPULARITER APPELATUS "TEL" FAMOSISSIMUM PRESENTATOR HIBERNICUS MULTORUM PROGRAMMORUM IN RADIO TELEVISIONEQUE NOTABILE COMPETITIONE EUROVISIONE ANNUALE CANTORUM PISSPOORUM EX NORVEGICAE ESTONIAQUE MALTAQUE ET GRANDE BRITANNICAE (NULLUS POINTUS MMIII). PATRONUS ET DUX "TOGORUM", SOCIETAS BOROS SEXUAGENARIANES IN BBC RADIO DUO CUM STICKEROS VEHICULENSIS "EGO SUM TOGGUS" PROCLAMAVERUNT. THATCHUM SUPERBUM CORONATUM SUSPICIONE UNIVERSALE WIGGUM. SALUTAMUS TERENTIUM WIGANENSIS. *(NONNE ERRATUM EDITORUS?)*   © LIMERICK UNIVERSITY

POLLY FILLER

On the Male Contraceptive Pill

COME on, girls, ask yourself this: would *you* trust your useless partner to remember to take the Pill? The same useless partner who can't remember your birthday or how to work the washing machine or where the cheese grater lives in the kitchen or what year his son is in at Tweedledums Nursery or the name of the au pair (Ndala for your information, Simon, not Uzbal who was the one before last and who came from a completely different war zone, ok?). Where was I? Oh yes… who can't remember to put the wheelie bin out on Tuesday evening or to record *Sex and the City* instead of *Australian Rules Backgammon* from Queensland presented by Paul Hogan and A.A. Gill or to put your dirty socks in the laundry basket which happens to be standing on the landing where it has been for the last five years…

DO you see what I'm getting at? Do you, girls? The only way the useless Simon would ever remember to take the male Pill was if it came in a can and tasted of lager! And even then he'd probably doze off in front of the television and spill it all over himself like he did last night! Remember, Simon? Probably not – which proves my point about men remembering things *exactly*!

Look, don't get me wrong. Men are good at remembering some things – like lying around and doing nothing. But as for anything else – forget it!!! Which is precisely what they would do with the Pill!!!!!

© *Polly Filler 2003.*

Lookalikes

Munster **McCartney**

Sir,
    I wonder whether David Blaine-baiter and sometime artist, poet and musician Paul McCartney has anything in common with man-made Herman Munster from the venerable American TV series The Munsters.
        Yours sincerely,
        ENA B. RUSHTON,
E. Twickenham.

New Tory Leader **Retiring Despot**

Sir,
    Readers may have already informed you, but... have you noticed the amazing resemblance between the new leader of the Tory party, Mahathir Mohamad, and the retiring despot prime minister of Malaysia, Michael Howard! There's something of the night about this, and we must be told.
        STEVE LEE,
Via email.

Wormtongue **Campbell**

Sir,
    Recent publicity surrounding the film and book "Lord of the Rings" leads me to remark upon the similarity between King Théoden's wise and loyal advisor Grima Wormtongue and our beloved prime minister's former press secretary Alastair Campbell. The similarity can only be physical, but one has to ask if by any chance they are related?
        Yours truly,
        TOM BLOOMFIELD,
Carmarthen.

Postman Pat **Byford**

Sir,
    Have your readers noticed the remarkable similarity between Mark Byford, Acting Director General of the BBC, and Postman Pat?
        Yours faithfully,
        ROGER PROTZ,
St Albans.

Portillo **Schwarzenegger**

Sir,
    Arnold Schwarzenegger = Michael Portillo?
        Yours,
        EDWARD MENDELBLAT,
Pinner, Middlesex.

Stringfellow **Mad Scientist**

Sir,
    I wondered whether Peter Stringfellow and the mad scientist painted by Joseph Wright could be in any way related? Obviously only good looks, and not madness, runs in the family.
        Yours sincerely,
        JOYCE CORSTON,
East Molesey, Surrey.

Higgins **Gollum**

Sir,
    While recently watching the snooker world championships, I realised how much Alex "Hurricane" Higgins resembled Gollum from the Lord of the Rings movies.
        DIANE SAMPSON,
Via email.

Perry **Rantzen**

Sir,
    Please find attached lookalikes of Grayson Perry (Turner Prize tranny guy) and Esther Rantzen. I think maybe Esther is Grayson's best work of art yet!
        LISA FRANKS,
Fishponds, Bristol.

Hutton **Meldrew**

Sir,
    Listening to the clipped tones of Lord Hutton delivering his report, I was struck by his vocal similarity to Victor Meldrew.
    "I don't believe it!" That was Victor's catchphrase. How appropriate.
    Are they by any chance related?
        MARTIN FOOKES,
Via email.

Lucan? **Lucan?** **Lucan?**

Sir,
    Have any of your readers noticed the resemblance between Jungly Barry, Billy Gibbons from ZZ Top and Archbishop Thomas Cranmer (not from ZZ Top)?
        Yours sincerely,
        ENA B. MANN,
London W2.

Beardsley **Crook**

Sir,
    Has anyone else noticed the startling similarity between Mackenzie Crook (Gareth Keenan in The Office) and the Victorian artist Aubrey Beardsley? Are their barbers related? I think we should be told.
        Yours faithfully,
        STAWELL HEARD,
London SE3.

Winner

Quaker

Sir,
I have noticed a startling similarity between a famous film director and the Quaker Oats man. Surely they are related in some form?
Calm down, dear!

Regards,
MARIA KEMP,
Glossop, Derbyshire.

Rumsfeld

Iliescu

Sir,
Am I the only one to have noticed the resemblance between Romanian President Ion Iliescu and US "Defense" Secretary Donald Rumsfeld? Have they ever been seen together? I think we should be told.

Yours,
BOB LADD,
Edinburgh.

Whitehouse

Blair

Sir,
Is it my imagination, but does Paul Whitehouse, starring in 'Happiness', bears a remarkable resemblance to Tony "Mr Happiness" Blair or do they just share the same dentist?
Yours faithfully,
ENA B. ANON.
London.

Scream

Johnson

Sir,
Has anyone else noticed the remarkable resemblance between Boris Johnson MP and Edvard Munch's 'The Scream'?
Apart from their hairstyles, could they be related?

Yours sincerely,
BRIAN LEEDHAM,
West Ewell, Surrey.

Andy   **Andy**

Sir,
Has anybody noticed the extraordinary resemblance between Andy Pandy and the BBC's political chap, Andrew Marr?
NAME AND ADDRESS WITHHELD.

Beethoven   **Short**

Sir,
I was struck by the remarkable similarity between the ideologically-challenged former cabinet minister Clare Short, pictured in the Guardian 1 March, and the well-known audio-logically-challenged composer Ludwig van Beethoven. Could they be in some way related, if only by their shared interest in listening devices? I think we should be told, as this is really bugging me.
Yours faithfully,
JOHN WILKERSON,
Barnsley, S. Yorks.

Moqtada

Mark

Sir,
I noticed this pair while flicking through the Telegraph. You never see Mark Steyn and Moqtada al-Sadr in the same room. Could the cool-headed man of peace and the bearded warmongering firebrand be, by any chance, related?
STEVE DUNTHORNE,
Blackpool.

Alice   **Marina**

Sir,
Have any of your other readers noticed the similarity between Marina Hyde (Guardian Diary contributor and columnist) and Alice (the rather thick one) from the esteemed 'comedy' programme the Vicar of Dibley. Are they related or indeed the same person? I think we should be told.

Yours faithfully,
SIMON EDWARD,
London SW9.

Beckett   **Mrs Tweedy**

Sir,
Is it me or does the Environment Secretary Margaret Beckett look like the wicked Mrs Tweedy from the film 'Chicken Run'?
MARTIN FOOKES,
Via email.

Brown

Shrek

Sir,
I was struck by the uncanny resemblance between our esteemed chancellor and the 'handsome' Shrek in the film Shrek 2. Surely Mr Brown isn't that much of an ogre?
MATT FENBY TAYLOR,
Via email.

Saddam   **Haddock**

Sir,
Given Saddam's propensity for using lookalikes, is there any possibility they have the wrong man? Something smells fishy in Baghdad!
SEAN COSGROVE,
Via email.

Powell   **Gaddafi**

Sir,
I have evidence that the recent historic meeting is nothing but a scam. I refer to the startling resemblance between Gaddafi and Robert Powell. We must be told!
Yours,
SIR EDWARD B. TEDWORTH,
Coventry.

News In Brief

MAN FAMOUS FOR SWEARING ON TV SWEARS ON TV SHOW HE WAS HIRED TO APPEAR IN BECAUSE HE MIGHT SWEAR SHOCK

A MAN whose rise to fame was based on his ability to swear on live television has shocked the nation by swearing on the TV show *'I'm A Celebrity, Get Me Out Of Here'.* *(Reuters)*

19-YEAR-OLD BOY GOES OUT FOR EVENING

by Our Entire Staff

A 19-year-old boy went out last night. He is believed to have had a drink and talked to some girls. *Reuters*

On Other Pages

- Why Harry Should Join the Army at Once by Sir Max Hastings **8**
- Good on Yer Harry! says TV's Lord Brocket **10**
- Can Staying up Late Lead to Tiredness? asks Dr Thomas Utterfraud **12**

GLENDA SLAGG

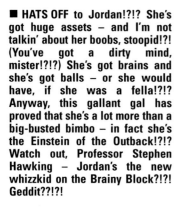

OUR BIRD IN THE BUSH!!! (GEDDIT?!)

■ HATS OFF to Jordan!?!? She's got huge assets – and I'm not talkin' about her boobs, stoopid!?! (You've got a dirty mind, mister!?!?) She's got brains and she's got balls – or she would have, if she was a fella!?!? Anyway, this gallant gal has proved that she's a lot more than a big-busted bimbo – in fact she's the Einstein of the Outback!?!? Watch out, Professor Stephen Hawking – Jordan's the new whizzkid on the Brainy Block?!?! Geddit??!?!

■ JORDAN – aren'tchasickof-her?!? This deformed dolly with the pneumatic knockers has been sendin' us all to sleep a-wigglin' and a-jigglin' in the jungle?!?! There's less to you than meets the eye, darlin'?!? Geddit?!? Put your ginormous jugs away and give us all a break, whydon'tcha?!?

■ *JORDAN?!?! Put a sock in it!?! Preferably one with a footballer inside it?!?! OK, so you've bedded* Becks!?!? Who hasn't?! Well, you haven't for a start!?!? And nor has anyone else except his lovely wife!?!? Put up or shut up, you Brainless Barbie with the Ballistic Bazookas!?!?

■ **JORDAN!?!? The gals of Britain salute you!?!? Feisty feminist icon and raunchy role model who** *(That's enough of this rubbish. Ed.)*

■ TED AND SYLVIA?!? Who cares?!? Why isn't it Ted and Jordan!?!?! That's the film we want to see!?!? *(You're fired. Ed.)*

■ HERE THEY ARE – Glenda's Valentine Valentinos:

● **Rock of Gibraltar** – OK, so he's a horse. But he's hung like a horse!?!? (Geddit?!?)

● **Jordan** – OK, she's a woman, but then women are the new men?!?!?

● **Sir Kevin Tebbit** – My kind of Mandarin!?!? Geddit?!?!

Byeeee!!!

BISHOP ATTACKS BLAIR

Et tu, Tutu?

"Your chosen subject is 'Programmes I don't watch'. Starting now... which part of Jordan's anatomy did Lord Brockett...?"

An Aldeburgh Taxi Driver Writes

Every week a well-known taxi driver discusses an issue of topical importance.

THIS WEEK: **Simon Bentley-Marchant,** proprietor of the Peter Pears Limousine Hire Co, Aldeburgh, Suffolk (Cab No. 1), gives his views on the new memorial sculpture to the late Benjamin Britten by Maggie Hambling, recently unveiled on Aldeburgh beach.

"I say, guvnor, that sculpture really is a bit of a shocker. Completely ruins the shoreline. I've got nothing against Ben Britten personally, but what's this shell got to do with anything? Don't get me wrong, it's not because, you know, he played for the other side, if you get my drift, and had a rather poor war, running off to America like that as soon as the first shot was fired, not to mention the fact that his music was, let's face it, unlistenable to, dreary operas about paedophiles and so on, no, it's the council I blame for allowing them to put up a thing like that in the first place. If you ask me, they should all be strung up, it's the only language they understand. I had that Maggie Hambling in the back of the limo once and I asked her not to smoke, 'f*** off' she said, that's the sort of people we get in Aldeburgh nowadays."

44

Why Bush Is The Real War Hero

O K, so Senator John Kerry fought in Vietnam and won a few medals. What is so heroic about that? Let's not forget that George Bush showed enormous courage by going to the dentist whilst he was in the Texas Home Guard. In my book, that shows Bush is the real war hero. And what was Kerry up to while Bush was risking his life for his country in the dentist's chair?

I'll tell you – this so-called Vietnam veteran was cosying up to peacenick traitor Jane Fonda in the hope of bringing down

Mark Steyn

the American Government.

And now we find out that Kerry had an affair with an intern according to the highly authoritative website *republicansmear.neo.con*. That doesn't surprise those of us who see Kerry for what he is – a yellow-bellied dope-smoking hippy! How long until we find out that he shot Kennedy when he was supposed to be killing Vietcong?

Not for cowardy Kerry the dangers of the Texan dentist's drill nor the hell of the peppermint-flavoured mouth-wash but *(You're fired. Brillo)*

That Goldsmith Legal Advice In Full

TOP SECRET – PRIVATE & CONFIDENTIAL

I, the Attorney General, Baron Goldsmith of Lincolns Inn, by the power invested in me by Her Majesty the Queen and her chief minister, being requested to pronounce on the legality or otherwise of the forthcoming war against Iraq, hereby do solemnly and verily give the following judgement:

1. It looks a bit dodgy legally to be honest.

2. But Alastair's dossier is jolly frightening, isn't it? Especially the 45 minutes bit.

3. Go for it! Bombs away!

Signed and sealed
Baron Goldsmith of Baghdad

PS. Will this do?

INQUIRY INTO INTELLIGENCE LAUNCHED

I'm sure I'll be cleared

LETTER FROM AMERICA *by Alistair Cook*

Cook: Good morning, yesterday was Super Bull Tuesday, the day when, as you know, the American primary season reaches its climax. The triumph of Senator Kerry in New Dworkin took me back to a balmy autumn day in 1932 and a golf course where I was playing a round with Senator Dewey, Governor Lewey and Judge Hewey. As I was preparing to drive off the seventh green, I spotted a lonely figure walking down the fairway looking for his ball in the large sand bunker for which that course is justly notorious. "Do you know who that is?" I asked my companions. "Why, that is our Uncle Donald," they quacked. As Bing Crosby once said to me, "Do you think I should give up now?" *(Continued for what seems like two hours)*

Announcer: And now, on the Archers, there's trouble down at the Old Fist And Gerbil as hundreds of Gay Rights Activists descend on Walter Gabriel's cottage for an all-day *(That's enough Radio Four. Ed.)*

COMMENT   THE TIMES MARCH 5 2004

Why My Cousin Will Be The Next President Of The United States

I WAS not at all surprised to discover that the man who is shortly to become the most powerful man in the world is closely related to me. Senator Kerry, whom many believe will soon be the President of the United States, is my 40th cousin, 27 times removed.

We share a common ancestor in Obadiah Twit, who was leader of the Puritan sect, the Loony Brethren, who fled to America in the early 17th century in the mistaken belief that Europe was about to be engulfed in a return of the Ice Age.

Twit established a colony on the banks of the Moggahogga River, but met an untimely end when a local Indian tribe, the Starbucks, grew impatient of his sermons, many of them lasting several days, and slaughtered Twit and all his followers in what went down in history as "The Loonies' Last Stand" (subsequently

William Rees-Mogg

used as the basis of the 1956 John Wayne classic *Massacre At Mogg Creek*).

When my cousin enters the White House, which given our shared ancestry must now seem inevitable, I look forward to inviting him over to the Garrick for luncheon, so that he can benefit from my advice on the conduct of world affairs, and possibly even to make the acquaintance of my son Jacob Really-Smugg, his 40th cousin 28 times removed, who, had it not been for a quirk of history, might well himself now be the President of the United States, rather than having been cruelly rejected by the inverted snobbery of the Kensington and Chelsea Conservative Association, who seem to believe that we Really-Smuggs are stuck-up snobs obsessed with our ancestry and our role in history, when in fact we are *(cont'd p.94)*

45

AN APOLOGY

WE MAY, in recent months, have given the mistaken impression through headlines such as "Smirking Asylum Seekers Bleeding Our Benefits System Dry" that asylum seekers were evil, smirking, individuals coming here to exploit our benefit system so as to live a life of astonishing luxury in Britain.

We now realise, in the light of the deaths of nineteen Chinese nationals cockle-picking off Morecambe Bay, that nothing could be further from the truth, and that asylum seekers are helpless, pathetic individuals exploited by evil gang-masters to live a life of horrific slavery here in Britain.

We apologise for any confusion caused, and any confusion in the future, when a group of Algerians are found huddled in the back of a lorry at Dover. We demand a stop to the flood of evil Smirking Asylum Seekers Bleeding Our... (cont. p. 94)

That Hilarious Ann Winterton Joke in Full

"Well there were these two Chinese men, no that's wrong, there were these two fish or were they sharks? Yes that's it, they were sharks and they were very hungry so one of them said to the other one 'I could murder an Indian', so they swam up to... was it Bradford? ...no I know, it wasn't an Indian at all, it was a Chinese meal they wanted so they went to that place where all the Chinese people died and one of the sharks said, 'Is this Eric Morcambe?' or perhaps that's what the other one said, anyway, they ended up eating cockles... oh dear, I think I've given away the punchline..."

Ann Winterton's Next Joke

Vote Conservative!

Ha!

Ha!

Ha!

Letters From The Late SIR JOHN GIELGUD

To The Late Lord Olivier OM

Dearest Larry,

I was horrified when I opened my Telegraph today to see that they've dredged up a lot of old letters which I must have written years ago to various boring people, most of whom even I can't now remember.

It really has come to something when a once-respectable newspaper like the Daily Telegraph (for which, you will remember, the great W.A. Darlington was once the theatre critic) is reduced to filling its pages with such appalling trivia as some note I wrote 60 years ago to the Inland Revenue asking them to be kind enough to wait a few more weeks for my cheque, as I had lent £50 to Ralph to pay for a weekend in Brighton with a new friend!

I must say, life up here gets rather tedious. So many of one's friends are in the other place. We were very honoured the other night, when we put on a performance of Sam Beckett's new play *Not Waiting For God Any More*, to see the Archangel Gabriel in the front row. He was looking radiant in *(cont. for the next 94 million years)*

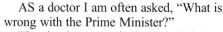

A Doctor Writes

Fibulation

AS a doctor I am often asked, "What is wrong with the Prime Minister?"

The simple answer is that Mr Blair is suffering from a routine condition amongst Prime Ministers – namely Fibulation or *Mendacious normalis bliarensis* to give it the full medical name.

What happens is that after a long period in office the Prime Minister begins to notice murmurs which may become more frequent and more pronounced as time goes on.

This gives rise to what is known as Fibulation or the compulsive telling of fibs. These may include lies on subjects as diverse as buying property in Bristol, or declaring war on Iraq or denying that there is anything wrong with him.

If you are worried about the Prime Minister there is nothing you can do about it.

© *A Doctor.*

"Don't you think it's time you let it go, Brian?"

1955 11 PLUS FAILURE

Cluff

MATHS CRISIS ROCKS GOVERNMENT

by Our Education Staff **G.C.S.E Reetayke**

TEACHERS today warned of a growing crisis in the higher levels of government as more and more politicians were "unable to do the basic arithmetic".

One teacher said, "There is a terrible shortage of numerate politicians and this has created a situation of declining standards in dealing with figures."

He continued, "We have reached a stage where the Education Secretary cannot equate a shortage of mathematics graduates with a £30,000 student debt at the end of three years."

Other mathematical howlers cited by teachers included some ministers who thought that *lowering* the pass mark in exams would *increase* educational standards and others who thought that doubling the number of exams every year would reduce the pressure on students.

The teacher concluded: "These are really elementary errors that one doesn't expect to see at this level but politics is so easy to get into nowadays that one shouldn't be surprised."

A government spokesman denied there was a problem. He said, "The suggestion that senior government ministers cannot handle figures is completely half-baked or half completely baked or possibly ⅔ baked over a third of the period, I'll have to get back to you on that."

SITTING ON THE DOCK OF ebay WASTING TIME....

ebay

grizelda

'SAME SEX MARRIAGE DOESN'T WORK' SAYS BUSH

by Our Man In Washington **Mary Whitehouse**

PRESIDENT Bush today lashed out at "unhealthy partnerships between men of the same sex", and pledged that he would ban any further attempts to formalise such "marriages" in the future.

"I myself", he said, "am guilty of forming such a special relationship with an English public schoolboy I met a few years back, but I can tell you, it all turned out badly.

Weapon of Ass Destruction

"It's all very well getting into bed with these guys, but when they want to kiss your ass and talk about sharing your toothpaste, it is time to draw the line."

It is believed that President Bush formed an unnaturally close friendship with a young British admirer, Tony Blair, 24, and that the two of them were on the phone to each other every day.

Blair told friends at the time that he would "go anywhere and do anything just to be with George", and he made several visits to Bush's Texan hideaway.

But later the relationship cooled, particularly when Blair began hanging around with a handsome German "friend" Gerhard, and his older French partner Jacques.

Donald Bumsfelt

The President added, "Some people feel that these relationships are blessed by God, but I can tell you that, in my experience, these so-called marriages never work out."

A spokesman for Mr Blair said that he was unavailable for comment because he was "too busy working on his plan to introduce top-up congestion changes for fat people."

Tony Blair is 19.

DEFENCE BUDGET CUT AGAIN

"Oh, all right then..."

'PASSION' OPENS TO STORM OF PROTEST

by Our Showbiz Staff **Bach Bamigboye** and **Johannes Ross**

A NEW version of the last days in the life of Christ has sparked a wave of controversy after its first performance in Leipzig last night.

B-Minor Mass Hysteria

The Passion, based on the gospel according to St Matthew, is filled with scenes of violence, and dwells at length on the blood-soaked last hours of Jesus, before he is brutally nailed to the cross.

Mel Gibson

Many of the audience left the church where the new work was premiered in tears, deeply moved by the horrendous scenes they had just sat through.

Jewish groups, however, were furious at Herr Bach's "outrageous anti-Semitism" and his inclusion of the chorus "His Blood Be Upon Us" sung by a group clearly identified as including many Jews.

Bach was unrepentant and told waiting newsmen that he was merely repeating what was written in the Bible, his favourite book.

St Matthew Parris

Other critics were angered by the decision to present the entire oratorio in German, instead of the original Aramaic.

"There weren't even any surtitles," said one furious English visitor. "I couldn't understand a word of it. It'll never catch on."

GIBSON DENIES ANTI-SEMITISM

I've been crucified by the Jews

"See the film!"   "Read the book!"

MEL GIBSON'S The Passion of The Christ

AJSinter (After Levin)

Notes & Queries

EXCLUSIVE TO ALL PAPERS

EATING McDONALD'S FOOD ISN'T GOOD FOR YOU!

On Other Pages

- Bears continue to defecate in woods **12**
- Sources close to the Pope say he's still a Catholic **15**

Advertisement

WAR WITHOUT FRONTIERS

The terrible events in Madrid... world shock... globalisation of terror... a message for us all... inflation of horror... nowhere is safe... terrible events... world shock... coming to terms with tragedy... hearts go out... shoulder to shoulder... united in common purpose... stand together at this time... who will be next?... let's hope it is someone else.

© All newspapers.

On Other Pages

● Why we should deny the terrorists the oxygen of publicity **2-94**

PROFESSOR TERRY RISTE, Professor of Terrorism Studies at the North London University of Terrorism (formerly The World of Leather, Brent Cross)

THIS latest attack in Spain has all the hallmarks of the regional separatist group TAPAS, or possibly the Islamic extremist group Al-Bran. However, we cannot rule out the possibility that a breakaway group, comprised of elements from both organisations, calling itself Al-TAPAS, may be responsible.

Nevertheless, an internet message from a spokesman, describing himself as Mohammed Al-Phoney, has claimed responsibility for yet another previously unknown group called HUMUS, middle-eastern terrorists with links to the Taramosalata Group and the Italian Red Pesto Brigade, who were responsible *(That's enough of this rubbish. Ed.)*

SHOCK NEW TESTS FOR 18-YEAR-OLDS

by Our Education Staff **Linda Chalk**

IN THE biggest shake up of secondary education since the last shake-up, the government has announced plans to scrap GCSEs, AS Levels and A Levels and to replace them with an all-purpose Educational Diploma.

Students at 18 will be confronted with a single exam paper which tests numeracy and literacy by asking the following two questions:

1. What is your name?
2. How old are you?

(Time allowed: 2 hours)

HOWARD 'TOO YOUNG' SAYS HEATH

THE FORMER Prime Minister, Sir Edward Heath, has attacked the Tory leader Michael Howard for being "too young".

Said Heath, "The modern Tory Party needs to be led by someone untainted by the Thatcher years, someone much older, perhaps with an agreeable house in Salisbury, a number of rich Chinese friends and an interest in music and sailing".

Grocer Heath is 94.

TV Highlights

Footballers' Wives

(ITV) Wednesday 9.00pm

In the most fantastically unbelievable plot so far, this episode sees a premier league footballer come home after training to spend the evening with his wife and children watching the television, before going to bed to get an early night so he's refreshed in the morning for the match.

ENGLAND RUGBY TEAM LOSES SHOCK

I've never met them in my life

ENGLAND CRICKET TEAM WINS SHOCK

I've always liked cricket

NO. 94
BARBARA AMIEL

You are said to have one of the largest collections of spoons in the world. Is it true?

Yes, I suppose I do have millions of spoons. Whole cupboards full of them.

Do you know how many you have?

I've no idea. I just keep on buying them. When you've got as many houses as we have, you've got to have rather more spoons than the ordinary person.

Are the spoons you buy very expensive?

Well, yes, I suppose they are. But we do entertain a lot, with presidents, prime ministers, world-famous artists and that kind of thing. So you have to have the best spoons money can buy.

Some people say that the shareholders money has been used to buy your spoon collection?

Typical small-minded British journalism. You people can't get anything right, can you? The shareholders begged me to buy those spoons, to make their grotty little lives more interesting.

How will you cope in prison?

The interview sadly ended at this point, before we could ask Lady Black whether anything amusing had ever happened to her in connection with a spoon.

NEXT WEEK: Lord Butler – "Me and My Butler".

Hopper: The Lost Self-Portrait

THOUSANDS OF UNQUALIFIED PEOPLE ENTER GOVERNMENT

by Our Asylum Staff **Oliver Letemin**

HUGE numbers of undesirable and unskilled workers have been allowed to enter the government without any checks being made on their suitability for the job.

This new scandal only came to light when a courageous whistleblower saw Immigration Minister Beverley Hughes being interviewed on Channel Four News.

Last Straw

"It was obvious," said the whistleblower, "that this woman knew nothing about anything. She was utterly useless. Why on earth was she allowed in and given a job?"

But government spokesman Jack Straw defended the policy. "We need useless people in government," he said, "to do the kind of work that competent people simply aren't prepared to do.

"You can't suddenly decide that you don't want useless people coming in any more. I myself am proud to say that I come from a useless background, and I like to think that my performance in office has justified our policy of not being too strict in checking whether people are any good or not."

Should These People Be Chucked Out And Sent Home? *You decide*

Beverley, 58
"I like it here in government. You don't have to be any good, and people accept you."

Ruth, 46
"I think useless people have a lot to contribute."

Baroness Amos
"Incompetent people have a different outlook on life, and can really mess things up in a way that others can't."

NEW IMMIGRATION SHOCK

You can't go around telling lies, Bev

...that's your job

The Daily Tsar

(Prop. Dirty Desmonski)

CZAR ELECTED IN 100% TURN OUT

by Our Man in Red Square **Andrew Marrx**

CZAR PUTIN the First romped home today in the Russian election against his unknown opponent Nobodski.

Said the Czar, "The Russian people have shown that they agree with my bribes *(surely policies? Ed)* and have embraced my election promise 'Vote for me or die'."

THOSE RESULTS IN FULL	
Omsk North	
KGB Putin (No relation)	2,738,402
NBG Nobodski (No votes)	0
No change	

ON OTHER PAGES ★ *Vote Putin and win a year's supply of potatoes 2 ★ Daily Recipe: Cabbage soup. Like your Grandma used to make before she was sent off to the Gulag 3 ★ PLUS sexy Tsar bird Putina Putinovitch (no relation) 4-94.*

"Bloody illegal immigrants..."

THE INSPECTOR MORSE MYSTERIES

— No. 94 —

THE CASE OF THE DEAD PRINCESS

(Red Jaguar is seen driving through leafy lanes of Gloucestershire. Cut to interior of vehicle)

Sergeant Lewis *(speaking over tape of The Marriage of Figaro)*: What I don't understand, sir, is why we're having to dig all this up again. We know it was just an accident...

Inspector Morse: Lew-is, Lew-is. Don't you learn anything? We're going to interview the Prince because we've been told to by the chief. And he's been told to send us by the bigwigs in London. Apparently, they want us to be "seen to be doing something". So belt up and keep driving, Lewis, it's not every day you get a chance to hobnob with Royalty.

Lewis *(taking out mobile)*: I'd better ring my wife and tell her I'm going to be late.

(Car is seen drawing up outside agreeable country mansion. Morse and Lewis are confronted by the dapper figure of Sir Alan Fitztightly)

Fitztightly: Oh, I suppose you are the two policemen we've been told to expect. His Royal Highness is in the Islamic Garden.

(Shot of Prince Charles bending over bed of nasturtium seedlings)

Charles: Come on, you little chaps, grow for Daddy.

Lewis *(sotto voce)*: He's a bloody nutter, sir.

Morse *(coughs and presents the Prince with his ID card)*: Excuse me, sir, Inspector Morse, Oxford CID. We'd just like to ask you a few questions about the death

of your late wife.

Charles *(to seedlings)*: Talk amongst yourselves, chaps. I've just got to have a word with these policemen. *(To Morse)* How can I help you, Inspector?

Morse: Well, sir, I'd like to know where you were on the night in question, 31 August 1997, between the hours of 10pm and 2.36am.

Charles: Oh, gosh, that's quite tricky! I, er, I must have my old diary somewhere. They keep them for me.

(Cut to Library. Red-faced Charles is

examining old leather-bound diary, while Lewis is spinning 15th-century globe in background)*

Charles: Oh, yes, here it is! Er, oh gosh...

Morse: Is something the matter, sir?

Charles: No, not at all. I see that I was with a, er, a friend that night.

Morse: So would this "friend" be able to confirm that you were not in Paris on that night?

Charles: I'm sure she, I mean he, I mean my friend, will...

(Cut to Snug Bar of The Old Trout, a famous Thames-side pub)

Lewis *(placing two foaming pints of Dexter's Old Peculiar on table)*: He's covering up for something, sir, isn't he? If you ask me, he's the one that did it.

Morse: Well, I'm not asking you, Lewis. Which is just as well, since he clearly *didn't* do it.

Lewis: Then what was he up to that night, that he got so red-faced about?

Morse: What do you think he was doing, Lewis? It's obvious.

Lewis: Sir, you don't mean he was...

Morse: Yes, Lewis, that is exactly what I mean. Now get me another pint of that Old Peculiar.

Lewis: So the whole thing's been a complete waste of time?

Morse: Not for me Lewis. You're driving.

(Final shot of the car driving back to Oxford. Morse has his eyes closed as he listens to Don Giovanni. To be repeated every week for next five years...)

LONDON TRANSPORT DISASTER

You wait ages for a bus and then three catch fire at once

Letter From Heaven

by Alistair Cooke

GOOD HEAVENS. I was sitting on my cloud talking to my old friend President Teddy Roosevelt, who asked me if I fancied a game of golf. It was a bright sunny day, as it always is up here, and I'd been told the course, laid out by Leonardo da Vinci, was better than St Andrews, although of course Saint Andrew himself, whom I was speaking to earlier, says he does not believe it. Where was I? Oh yes, in heaven, waiting for my first harp lesson from my very old friend, the late Harpo Marx. But then, up here, we are all of us late *(Continued for eternity)*

GLENDA SLAGG

FLEET STREET'S QUEEN OF THE QUILL!

■ HATS OFF to Des O'Connor, the 72-year-old Dad-to-be!!?! OK, so he's old enough to be his own great-grandfather – but so what?!? You don't have to be a teenager to change nappies and wheel the pram round the park, do ya?!?! Come off it, Mr Newsman – you're just jealous 'cos Dishy Des has got a leggy lovely up the duff!?!? Good on yer, Des!?!?!

■ GOO-GOO ga-ga!?!? And that's just what Dirty Des O'Connor will be saying when he's a-droolin' and a-dribblin' and his poor little 'un has to help him go to the toilet and wheel him round the park in his bathchair!!?!?! What a Desgrace!?!? (Geddit?!?) At your age you should be in the garden putting in a few bulbs and not upstairs putting your you-know-what into you-know-where!!?!? Clear off, Des!?!? I said "Clear off, Des" – or haven't you got your hearing aid turned on!?!?!

■ BLIMEY!?! Have you seen Anne Robinson?!?! One minute she looks like Barbara Cartland, the next she looks like Barbie Doll!?!? Give us the name of your plastic surgeon, luv, and I'll make a point of avoiding him!!?! You are the *weirdest* link! Goodbye!!?!

■ ANNE ROBINSON – doesn't she look a million dollars?!?!? Or at least that's what she must have paid Dr Strangeface to get her ears put up by her knees – or whatever she's had done!?!?! Believe me, darlin', you don't look bad for a 60-year-old – you look awful!?!?!! Goodbye!?!?!!

■ WHICH 60-year-old wouldn't die to have the little girl looks of the *Princess of the Putdown!?!?!?* I mean sexy Anne Robinson, stoopid!?!?! Perhaps she and Des O'Connor should get together and start a family!?!?!!? His **link** is anything but weak!?!?!! Geddit!?!?!

■ HERE THEY ARE – Glenda's Easter Hunnies!?!?! (Geddit?!?)

● **TV's Simon Kelner** – Here's an Independent gal who wants the big one, not the compact version!?!! Geddit?!?!

● **Sir Menzies Campbell** – They call you Ming, I'll call you anytime?!?! Mmmm-ing!!?!?!

● **Alastair Ross** – the Mucky Major!!?! At last a Hussar who isn't Gay!?!?! How about some under-cover manoeuvres round at my place?!?!?!

Byeeeee!!!

DES O'CONNOR TO HAVE NEW JOKE

by Our Showbiz Staff Lunchtime **O.A.P.**

DES O'CONNOR, the 72-year-old entertainer, has astonished friends by revealing that he is going to have a new joke.

O'Connor already has three jokes, aged 53, 42 and 38, and most showbiz experts thought that he was too old to have another.

Some claimed it was undignified for a man of 72 to try for another joke. Said one, "There's a real chance that Des will die on stage. And what will happen to the joke then?

"Will it end up being taken care of by Little and Large? It doesn't bear thinking about."

But a delighted O'Connor was unapologetic and declared, "This shows that even at my age I've still got lead in my pencil – and I've used it to write a new joke."

Have you got Aids?

Yes, they told me to pose with you

---

by Our Showbiz Staff **Lunchtime O'Bit**

FOLLOWING the death of Sir Peter Ustinov, 86, the humanitarian and international diplomat, tributes from admirers flooded in from all over the world.

Among the first was a message from the late Josef Stalin, "Peter was a great friend to Russia, and a great friend to me. His staunch support of everything we had tried to achieve in the Soviet Union was a real comfort in the dark days of the Cold War."

Another admirer, the late Mao-Tse-Tung, said, "Peter was a great friend to the Chinese People's Republic, or at least those left after I'd killed most of them."

"What we in the Politburo particularly remember him for was his marvellous gift for impersonating a trombone – or was it a racing car?"

Others who queued up to pay their respects to the Great Impersonator included former President Milosevic, Saddam Hussein and Mr Osama bin Laden, who said that nothing had inspired him more in his crusade for universal rights than Ustinov's incomparable portrayal of the Emperor Nero in the film *Quo Vadis*.

On Other Pages Was 'Renaissance Man' Ustinov The Greatest Painter Since Leonardo?

"Is it me or is Anne Robinson getting younger?"

Nursery Times

☺ **Friday, 19 March, 2004** ☺

JACK GETS GO-AHEAD TO PLANT MAGIC BEANS

by **The Brothers GM**

THE GOVERNMENT last night gave Jack the green light to cultivate his controversial genetically-modified beans.

Environmentalists have voiced concerns that the GM beans would produce a massive beanstalk which would grow up to the sky and which would result in a horrible giant coming down with an axe.

Scientists, however, were quick to pour scorn on what they called "alarmist nonsense, the stuff of fairytales".

Late News

Defence Cuts – Grand Old Duke of York to have one hundred men only. *"I don't think I'll be marching them up or down any hills,"* he said, *"because they haven't got any boots."*

THE BOOK OF SHARON

Chapter 94

1. And lo, there was dwelling in the land of Gaza a holy man of the Hamas-ites, whose name was Yas-sin, which is to say the man of death.

2. And Yas-sin was old and full of years, and his beard was extremely white, like unto the snow on Mount Arafat.

3. And Yas-sin was sore afflicted, so that he could not walk, but needeth many followers to carry him hither and thither on a small chariot which is called an "wheelchair".

4. And despite these afflictions, Yas-sin plotted darkly in his heart against the children of Israel, conspiring how he might smite them.

5. But Yas-sin had one problem.

6. For the children of Israel had many tanks and guns and many rockets, even unto the device that is nuclear.

7. For thus had revealed the prophet Vanunu in the *Times that is Sunday*, for which he had been locked up by the children of Israel.

8. But that is another story.

9. Thus when it came to the smiting, it was a bit one-sided.

10. So Yas-sin spake unto the sons and daughters of the Araf-ites, saying unto them "Go forth into the land of Israel and slay all the men, women and children of that land, and yourselves also.

11. "For it hath been revealed to me that whosoever doeth this shall be taken straightway into Paradise, where many virgins will be waiting, even a-gagging for it.

12. "This doth not of course apply to the daughters of Ham-as, but you can't have everything."

13. And they did as they were bidden, and so it came to pass, even as Yas-sin had foretold, save for the Paradise bit.

14. And when Sharon saw what the sons and daughters of the Hamas-ites had done, he waxed wroth.

15. Boy, did he wax wroth.

16. Then said Sharon, "Woe unto the Hamas-ites, for have I not smitten them again and again, like unto the hammer that falleth repeatedly upon the anvil?

17. "Have I not laid waste their dwellings with the great Bull of Dozer?

18. "And have I not built a mighty wall round the land of Israel (not to mention a few bits of Palestine as well) that is 50 cubits high and 50 cubits wide and 10,000 cubits long.

19. "And still they learneth not the lesson. They come like a wolf in the night, to devour our lambs in the fold.

20. "For it is many years that I have smitten the Hamas-ites, the Araf-ites, the Hezboll-ites and all the other -ites in vain."

21. "So the time hath come to try an new approach – I shall smite them even harder."

22. And so Sharon rose early and girdeth up his loins and did send his ships that are called "gun" (a gift from the Land of Dubya).

23. And thus did the children of Israel seek out Yas-sin, even as he was at his prayers, giving thanks for the number of Israelites that had been slain.

24. And they slew him, along with any men, women and children who happened to be standing nearby. And when he saw this Sharon rejoiced and the heart of Sharon exulteth at this slaughter.

25. "This will teach the Hamas-ites a lesson they will never forget," he saith.

26. And, lo, the sons of the Arab-ites rose up in their thousands, even their tens of thousands, and crieth aloud, "Woe unto Sharon and the children of Israel. We will teach them a lesson such as they will never forget."

27. Then they went forth to seek out the children of Israel, that they might slay them.

28. And thus yet again did Sharon return in his wisdom to the square that is called one. *(Continued to the end of time or the Day of Judgement, which ever shall be the sooner.)*

NEW ARMY SHOCK

I don't know about body armour, but a shirt and a gun would be useful

"There's not much finesse about big game hunting these days"

POETRY CORNER

In Memoriam The 11th Duke Of Devonshire

So. Farewell
Then Your
Grace
As I believe
Is the correct etiquette
When addressing
A Duke.

But why were you
The Duke Of Devonshire
When you lived
In Derbyshire?

This is a mystery
Which cannot be
Resolved
In a short poem
Of this
Kind.

    The 11th E.J. Thribb (17½)

In Memoriam Milton Shulman (90), famous theatre critic

So. Farewell
Then Milton
Shulman

Doyen of
Drama critics

Yours was a
London run
Beaten only
By the Mousetrap

But now
The curtain
Has fallen

And we
Are going off
To catch the
Last train
Home.

    E.J. Thribb (17½)

MODERN NURSERY RHYMES

Tracy, put the telly on (x3)
We'll watch some vids.

Suki, turn it off again (x3)
Too violent for the kids.

Tom, Tom, the burglar's son,
Mugged a bloke and away he run.
The cops gave chase,
Took him down their place,
Where he topped himself with
         a trainer lace.

Jack Sprat eats lots of fat,
His wife eats lots of sweeties.
He has had a coronary,
She has diabetes.

In Memoriam Morris McWhirter, founder of *The Guinness Book Of Records*

So. Farewell
Then Norris
McWhirter

Founder of *The Guinness Book of Records*.

Your book sold
So well it
Got into
Itself.

But sadly, at 78,
You personally did
Not set any
Records in
The "World's Oldest
Man" section.

    E.J. Thribb (17½),
the world's second-
youngest published
free-verse poet
(not including China)

In Memoriam Ray Charles, famous singer and pianist

So. Farewell
Then Ray
Charles

Famous singer
And pianist.

You invented
"Soul".

One of your most
Famous songs was
'Hit The Road Jack'

And now, sadly,
You won't
Come back
No more
No more
No more
You'll never come back
No more.

    E.J. Thribb (17½)

Lines On The Discontinuation of Nigel Dempster's Diary in the *Daily Mail*

So. Farewell
Then sixty-two-
Year-old Sherborne-
Educated diarist,
Formerly married to
The Lady Camilla, third
Daughter of the
Eleventh Duke of
Leeds, and third
Cousin, twice-removed, of
Her Late
Majesty, Queen
Elizabeth The Queen
Mother,
Currently being
Comforted, close
Friends tell me
By *(That's enough of this
poem. Ed)*

E.J. Thribb, the
17½-year-old, Tooting-
Comprehensive-educated son
of the late Doris Thribb, the
third daughter of Hezekiah
Thribb and close friend of
Keith and his mother
(I said that's enough. Ed.)

In Memoriam Marlon Brando

So. Farewell
Then Marlon
Brando,
Method actor and
Hollywood legend.

"Mumble mumble
Mumble."

Yes. That was
Your catchphrase.

E.J. Thribb (17½)

Also Farewell
Then, Anthony Buckeridge,
Creator of *Jennings*.

"Fossilized fish-hooks!"
Yes, that was
Your catchphrase.

But now you
Have been
Sent to see
The Great Beak
In the sky.

Cave God!

E. 'Jennings' Thribb (11½)

MODERN NURSERY RHYMES

Jack and Jill went up the hill
In a four-wheel drive they'd nicked.
Did handbrake turns among the ferns
Then torched the car for kicks.

Doctor Foster went to the Costa
In the south of Spain,
Drank some sangria and litres of beer
And went back again and again.

Bobby Shaftoe's
gone to sea,
When he comes
back he'll have
VD,
Like as not he'll
give it to me,
Bonny Bobby
Shaftoe.

In Memoriam Sydney Carter, hymnwriter

So. Farewell
Then Sydney
Carter,
Author of *The Lord
Of The Dance.*

Keith and I
Remember
Singing it at
Assembly.

"I danced in the da-da
Da-da-da-da
Da
Dum-dum-da-da-da-
Da-da-dum-di-dum"

Unfortunately there is
Insufficient space
To recall the whole
Of your most famous
Hymn.

E.J. Thribb (17½),
"Lord Of The Verse"

In Memoriam "Spot", The First Dog

So. Farewell
Then Spot,
English Springer
Spaniel, loyal friend
And companion
To President George W.
Bush
For fifteen
Years.

Keith says
You were nearly as
Faithful
As the English poodle
Blair.

I had to point
Out to him that
Poodles are
French –
Which spoiled
His joke.

My joke was that
Bush and Blair were
The dogs of war.

But Keith did
Not find this
Funny
As he considers the
War is a serious
Matter.

E.J. Thribb (17½)

TOP TERRORIST WAS MODEL PUPIL Says Headmaster

by Our Education Staff **John Clare de Loon**

"ST CAKES has never had a more charming and responsible student."

That was the verdict of the £48,000-a-term top independent school's headmaster, R.J. Kipling, when told that the former head boy Iqbal Ahmed Fotherington-Hatterjee had been arrested on charges of plotting to blow up the world.

Alma Martyr

Said Kipling, "Eekie, as we knew him, did very well in his A-levels, achieving 'A Stars' in Chemistry, Biology and Nuclear Studies.

"He also won the A.N. Wilson Scripture Prize for an outstanding essay on 'Why The Infidel West Must Be Destroyed'.

"He was a keen hockey player, turning out for the Second Eleven, and he played the clarinet in the School Orchestra's performance of *Oh What A Lovely Holy War*.

"I cannot believe that Eekie would be involved in anything like blowing up the world, and the news that he was found in possession of a bag of chemical fertiliser has come as a great shock to us all.

"Clearly it was his friend Faisal (Jihad's, 1991-96) who the police should be looking for."

Do you find this article offensive to Britain's ethnic minorities? If so, we'd like to hear from you.

If you wish to join the debate, email your message now to wastepaperbinladen@blowup.uk

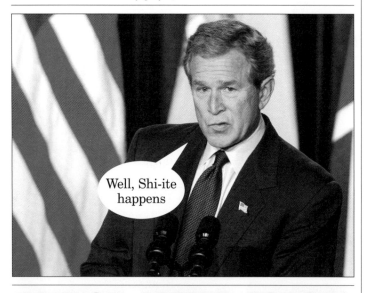

Well, Shi-ite happens

BRITISH ARMED FORCES TO BE CLOSED DOWN
Blair To Take 'Personal Charge'

by Our Defence Staff **Brigadier Trumper-Smythe**

SERVICE chiefs were outraged last night by the government's proposals that the armed forces must be modernised by closing them down completely.

Said the prime minister, "In the 21st Century it really is a bit out of date to have soldiers running around with guns and tanks and that sort of thing. And it is not as though we go to war all the time – only every few months.

"Anyway," Mr Blair went on, "people are getting this all out of proportion. We are merely cutting a few items, such as the army, the navy and the air force."

What's Wrong With Charles Kennedy? YOU Decide!

a) He is an alcoholic wreck.

b) He is a crack cocaine addict.

c) He is dying of AIDS.

d) He is the Leader of the Liberal Democrats and we don't want you to vote for him.

Kennedy: Two shots

Can you remember where you were when you heard the news that Kennedy was dead drunk?

Phone now on 09997 42873 and win the next election!

Phone the Daily Mail now on 09997 42873 and share your memories!

A Liberal Democrat Doctor Writes

AS A Liberal Democrat doctor, I am often asked, "Doctor, you were sacked by Charles Kennedy. Can you give us an objective medical opinion about his drunkenness?"

The simple answer is, "Try and stop me."

What happens is that the doctor, or *Hades furia femina scornata,* to give her the full medical name, makes a diagnosis based on the following symptoms: an excess of bile and an enlarged spleen.

This causes the doctor to speculate that Charles Kennedy is a washed-up old soak who should resign at once and make way for a more talented member of the Liberal Party – possibly one with medical qualifications.

If you are worried about Charles Kennedy, you should consult a newspaper at once.

© A. Dr Jenny Tonge

Exclusive To All Newspapers

HASH KENNEDHY GOT A DRINKSH PROBLEM?

by **Lunchtime O'Booze**

I SHAY thish (hic), Charles Kenner... Kenner... anyway... he'sh pished 24/7... I wash told this by a very good source... I can't remember hish name or indeed mine... but talking of source, I'll have another large one... zzzzzz

© Phil Glass, Pot & Kettle Productions.

"Wait! Before we go into the Joneses for dinner... what's our exit strategy?"

21-YEAR-OLD HAS GIRLFRIEND

by Our Entire Staff **Phil Space**

A 21-year-old student may have a girlfriend, it emerged last night.
Reuters

ON OTHER PAGES ● *Girl's Father Owns House* **5** ● *Girl Went To School* **6** ● *Girl Has A Friend* **8** ● *Why Oh Why Won't The Press Leave Prince William Alone?* **94**

"...and just why kids today are obsessed with sex is beyond me"

GARDENERS' QUESTION TIME
With Old John Prescott

1st Caller: What is the best thing to do with my lawn?

Old John: This is the time of year for getting rid of all that awful grass and putting in some housing instead.

1st Caller: But, John, I don't really want a house in my back garden.

Old John: Fair enough. Then put in a block of flats. They come up nicely and they have the added advantage of being perennial. In fact, you'll never get rid of them.

2nd Caller: Hello, John. I'm having trouble with weeds.

Old John: Me, too. They keep saying we don't need millions of houses all over the countryside.

2nd Caller: So, how do you deal with them?

Old John: I ignore them completely. I just get on with it and start digging those foundations.

3rd Caller: What sort of plant would you recommend for an English country garden?

Old John: Heavy industrial plant, concrete mixers, earth movers, bulldozers and *(cont. 94 MHz)*

A Manager Writes

AS a manager, I am often asked, "Manager, where are all the doctors?" The simple answer is, "There aren't any – we've spent all the money on new managers."

What happens is that the National Health Service gets its priorities in a condition known medically as *Rectum supra mammarium* (or *Arse-over-tit*, to give it the colloquial name).

The symptoms include an outbreak of paperwork, a rash of targets and a resultant increase in management which may develop into a more serious build-up of bureaucracy with the inevitable haemorrhaging of money and total collapse of the system.

If you are worried about the increase in NHS bureaucracy, you should complain in triplicate to the Deputy Manager of the Management of Managers Department, The Management Centre, Management House (formerly St Saviour's Hospital, London).

© *A. Manager*

THE TIMES

WORLD EXCLUSIVE

Figures Show That Giving Teenagers Access To Contraception Means They'll Have Sex With One Another

ON OTHER PAGES

Experts say that releasing bears into woodland area increases chances of them defecating there by 100% **page 7**

Researchers suggest that the appointment of a new Pope leads to increase by one in the overall number of Catholic Popes **page 10**

THIS WEEK

LUCIAN FREUD

As the most distinguished living artist in Britain, you have never before consented to give an interview. We are therefore very privileged that you should have granted us this unprecedented opportunity to question you about spoons. May I first ask you, as someone who has painted many of the best-known figures of our time, such as the Duke of Devonshire and Andrew Parker Bowles, has the depiction of spoons ever become a significant theme in your work?

I take it from your silence that you are not prepared to discuss this point... Could I then put it another way? In your recent portrait of Her Majesty the Queen, you showed only her head. Whereas another artist, say, Sir James Gunn, had no inhibition in showing a full-length study of the Royal Family, sitting round at tea-time, holding cups of tea with spoons in them. Did you consider that a picture of this type was too banal?

OK, can I put it another way? Now that you are 80, do you still manage to shag all these women you paint?

I was going to ask you if anything amusing had ever happened to you in connection with a spoon, but now that you've left the room that seems rather pointless.

NEXT WEEK: Anna Ford – *"Me And My Ford"*

Lines Written On The Announcement Of A Possible Rift In The Marriage Of Mr And Mrs David Beckham

BY WILLIAM REES-MCGONAGALL

'Twas in the year two thousand and four
It was reported that the Posh and Becks marriage
                                    might be no more.
There was soon no other topic of conversation
Through every stratum of the British nation.

To all those who said that Becks had been unfaithful
                                    to his Posh,
England's brave captain retorted merely that this
                                    was 'Tosh'.
But, alas for his claims that there was nothing
                        between him and Miss Loos,
A series of text messages appeared in the *News
                        of the Screws*.
Readers spent their Sunday trying to decipher
                                    the blanks
Where words had been erased, such as c*** and w***s.

Long on their pencils the fans did suck
To establish whether the pair had gone as far as a f***
*(That's enough of this filth in a family satirical
magazine. Ed.)*

Did you find this poem offensive? We would like to hear your views. If you want to join the debate, please send us a text message saying what you would like to do to someone else, such as Sandra in Human Resources.

ON OTHER PAGES: Why am I not allowed to read the above article just because I am only 5? by Peaches Geldof (exclusive to the *Peach Sundae Telegraph*)

Those Disgusting Beckham Text Messages In Full

PRIVATE EYE can now reveal the complete sordid conversation that took place between England's top editor Andy Coulson and former PR girl Rebecca Loos with whom Coulson developed a passionate relationship in Madrid.

AC: I want t**ts! I want t**ts with s*x in them! I'm gagging for it – go on fill up my organ!

RL: Ok, we've got b**king, we've got sh*gging, we've got w**king. Is that good for you?

AC: I'm so excited. I'm jumping around. Do you want me to talk m*n*y to you?

RL: Yeah. I'm feeling really gr**dy. Get out your big ch*q**!

AC: How do you want it?

RL: Straight in my b**k account. I can't wait any longer.

AC: Three hundred gr**d?

RL: I'm f**thy rich!

AC: And I'm just f**thy!

© *N*ws of the Scr*ws*

Loos woman

Rebekah – A Woman Obsessed With Sex

THE shy, retiring "other woman" at the centre of the Beckham row has been described by friends as "a voracious sexaholic determined to bring down a top sportsman".

According to these close friends, Rebekah Wade, the Editor of the *Sun*, is a manipulative and obsessive stalker of celebrities who has long had her eye on Beckham and wants to split up his marriage so that *(cont. p. 94)*

HOW THE FOREIGN PAPERS SAW THE BIGGEST STORY IN THE WORLD

Martian Times

XXRGLL GRZLL XRXXGL
BECKS YRRRX POSH BCXY
YZGLGK XRGLLG RXXGLL

by XRRRL ZZZLOGZ

POSH aaagll Becks xllzelz xrxxel xrgllg xllrrrg Posh xlllrge aaxllg xxllggr Becks zzrrge.

On Other Zgrllxss
● Xrllziig ● Zzloxccez ● Xynljr
● Arrzxx ● Xzerll ● Iraq.

We're staying together for the sake of the money

gnomafone™

A Statement From The Chairman

THE distressing news that Mr and Mrs Beckham's marriage is in trouble will inevitably give rise to queries about the suitability of the England captain as the public face of Gnomaphone.

Is he an ideal role model for impressionable young persons to look up to?

The answer is unequivocal – Yes. Mr Beckham and his friend Ms Loos have demonstrated beyond question the usefulness of our telecommunications devices for sending obscene messages speedily and effectively. They have proved that we at Gnomaphone have pioneered exciting new technologies for the 21st Century to revolutionise personal relationships on an intimate basis.

Far from distancing ourselves from Mr Beckham, we would like to endorse his imaginative response to the possibilities of exploring the digital age.

gnomafone™
Pay as you ***k!

GLENDA SLAGG

FLEET STREET'S **** *****!!

■ HATS OFF to Posh Spice!!?! You've gorra be kiddin', mister!?!?! No wonder her handsome hubby has ditched her and gone off a-sexin' and a-textin' the sexy senoritas of Old Madrid!?!? And for why?!?! Because Not-Very-Posh is a whingein' washed-up has-been with fake tits and a facelift!?!? No offence, Victoria, but Aunty Glenda tells it like it is?!?!?!

■ POSH SPICE!?!? Don'tchajust-hateher?!?!? Of course her bloke's gone out a-stonkin' and a-bonkin' in Sunny Spain, the love capital of the world!?!? What hunky full-blooded central midfielder wants to spend his nights alone whilst his selfish scarecrow of a missus is trying to resurrect her sad solo career five million miles away!?!? Good on yer, Becksy!?! Give Miss Madrid one for Aunty Glenda!?!?! Geddit???!?

■ POSH SPICE – she had it coming to her!?!?! Wanna know the truth?!?! I hate her. And I'll tell you something else – I hate her even more!!?!?

■ HERE THEY ARE – Glenda's April Phwoars?!?!?

● David Beckham – They think it's all legover!?!? And it is!?!?! Geddit?!?

● Becks – Here's a message from Aunty Glenda!? I've got no knickers on!!?!?

● The England captain – Come and get your free kicks round my place, Senor Sex?!?! Geddit!?!?! And leave your wife at home because I hate her!!?!? *(See above)*

Adiosssss!!!

"They've really made 'Friends Reunited' easy to use"

TOP PRIEST'S SENSATIONAL KISS-AND-TELL REVELATIONS

I Told Charles, 'Make An Honest Woman Of Camilla'

Continuing Our Exclusive Serialisation Of The Scandalous Memoirs Of **George Carey**, former Archbishop of Canterbury

AS PART of my pastoral remit, I felt it my duty to lend my assistance over the vexed problem of the relationship between His Royal Highness, the Prince of Wales, and his longtime companion Mrs Parker Bowles. On the one hand, they were clearly a loving couple in a long-term stable relationship. On the other, Prince Charles would one day be the Head of the Church, and he was a divorced man who might marry a divorced woman. This was a tricky one which I never managed to resolve.

Tomorrow: Gay bishops – another tricky one I didn't manage to resolve; falling congregations – yet another tricky one *(see above)*

THOMAS *THE PRIVATISED TANK ENGINE*

BY THE REV. TAWDRY

THE Fat Controller was looking very happy with himself.

"Why are you so happy," asked Colin the Cancelled Train, "when you've made huge losses and failed all the punctuality targets?"

"Not *all* the targets," beamed the Fat Controller. "We can still make something arrive on time. Look – here comes my bonus!"

And at that moment a huge cheque came into the platform.

"Hurrah!" said the Fat Controller. "Now I can buy a car!"

NEXT WEEK: Ronald The Replacement Bus breaks down again.

Daily Tripoligraph

2 Barrels of Oil

GADDAFI SALUTES 'BRAVE' BLAIR

by Our Man In Tripoli **Libya Purves**

COL GADDAFI has taken a bold political gamble by agreeing to meet the notorious Western war criminal Tony Blair.

Said Gaddafi last night, "I know in the past Blair has become something of a pariah among the civilised nations. Many have refused to deal with him after his acts of terrorism in Iraq and the thousands of deaths which have resulted from his crazed lust for power.

"But it is my belief now," the Libyan spiritual leader and world statesman continued, "that it is time to bring Blair in from the cold, and to draw a line under his unfortunate international record."

Gaddafi Duck

But some Libyan peace groups were furious at their government's attempt to rehabilitate Tony Blair so soon after his Iraq aggression.

"Blair is a dangerous lunatic who believes that he is infallible," said spokesman Tony Benn-Ghazi. "He is totally unpredictable and should not be trusted to buy our oil and give us a huge amount of money."

NEW MIDDLE-EAST DEAL

This is very nice wallpaper

OK, I sell it to you $20 a roll... okay, to you, my friend, $15... is good price

On Other Pages

★ *This week's public hangings: where to see them* **14** ★ *Was Blair responsible for Lockerbie crash?* **8** ★ *Tent prices tumble – is this the end for civilisation?* **10** ★ *Your camel trains tonight* **24**

School news

St Cakes

Hadj Term begins today. There are 798 boys and no girls in the school on the instructions of the new Imam *(see below)*. M. Hussain (Fatwa's) is Keeper of the Fertiliser. N.J.Q. Burkas-Peerage (Mecca's) is succeeded by P.F. Halal-Butcher (Hamas's). The Rev. P.J. Gropetrouser, our former Chaplain, has been replaced by Mohammed Al-Sadr as the School Imam. The Classics Department has been closed down and replaced by Koranic Studies (nine periods a day) to be led in the School Mosque (formerly St Cake's Chapel) by the Ayatollah Rasfanjani from Iran. The Camel Race will be run on the Field of the Prophet (formerly St George's Meadow) on 1 May 1572. There will be a performance of the musical *Saladin Days*, directed by Ned El-Sherrin O.C., on 16 June 1572. Speech Day is on 8 July 1572, main speaker: HRH Prince Charles on "Our Debt To Islam" (£200 billion). Executions will be on 12 July. Tickets from the Bursar, Col. Fotherington-Gaddafi, O.C., c/o The Old Tent, Sandy Lane, New Riyadh, Solihull.

"I'm keeping you busy while my mates bulldoze your home"

POLLY FILLER

SORRY, Gwyneth – you've blown it! Any hopes you had of playing *me* in the forthcoming film of my best-selling book *Mummy For Old Rope* by Polly Filler, have just gone out of the window! How could you say, recently-pregnant Ms Paltrow, that mothers shouldn't work and should stay at home and look after their children?

It's a well-known fact that working mothers are much *better* mothers than the stay-at-home neurotics, because their children turn out independent, challenging and fluent in Estonian – thank you Cskurg, our brilliant new au pair who arrived on May 1st!

And not only do we working mums allow our children the freedom to bond with a variety of teenage immigrants from cultures as diverse as Iraq and Colombia, but our very absence at work means that our children are more pleased to see us at the end of the day before we go out to the theatre or dinner!

In fact, Charlie, our funny, energetic four-year-old, loves to play games with me, asking me who I am and quizzing Cskurg about who the strange woman is in the living room!!!

BUT above all, Gwyneth, love, you'll only know what motherhood is *really* about when you realise you haven't got just one baby but two! Wait till your bloke from Coldplay is slobbing in the next room watching 'Underwater Quadbiking from Okinawa' on Granada's Frogmen and Motors Channel (like a certain useless partner I could mention but I won't, to spare Simon's blushes).

Then Gwyneth, dearie, you'll suddenly find yourself desperate to go out to work – but you won't be able to. And you know why? Because I won't cast you as Polly in my brilliant new film, as I'll have offered the part to Kate Winslett! (Fine actress and sensible working mum!!)

Sorry! And good luck with the going mad alone in the kitchen with the screaming, puking infant and the bottle of white wine!!

© *Polly Filler.*

ARCHBISHOP SLAMS BLAIR OVER IRAQ

by Our Chief War Correspondent **Lunchtime O'Basra**

BRITAIN's top Primate, the Rt. Rev. Rowan Beardie, last night launched an astonishing personal attack on the Prime Minister, Tony Blair, over his handling of the Iraqi war.

The Archbishop's outspoken comments provoked a storm of protest and outrage in Westminster, as MPs rallied to support their beleaguered leader as he wilted under the savage assault delivered from the pulpit of Canterbury Cathedral earlier in the day.

Exit Pursued By A Beard

Leading churchmen also expressed disquiet over the Archbishop's controversial intervention in the political arena – many of them expressing fears that he had "gone too far" in his blunt denunciation of Britain's elected head of government.

As the furore showed no signs of abating, informed observers were last night predicting that one of the two men would have to resign.

That Astonishing Beardie Sermon In Full

"In a modern environment, the old paradigm of trust in a political context has been deconstructed in such a way as to obfuscate and blur over our understanding of – and our obedience to – the imperatives, both human and non-human, which create the moral dynamic which is an essential underpinning of any attempt to create that genuine structure of acceptance which St Augustine of Hippo rightly regarded, in my view, as the basis for what he called 'katagnorosis'. And now, Hymn 94."

● How shocked were you by the Archbishop of Canterbury's attack on the Prime Minister's Iraq policy? If you want to join the great 'Beardie v. Blair' debate, you can contact us through **www.blairbeardrow.co.uk**

Bush Cassidy And The Sunsays Kid

EPIC western in which two mismatched outlaws wisecrack their way through a series of disasters before coming to a sticky end.

If you would like to see the above film or just join the great film debate, simply log on to www.dubya.con

---

DIRTY DEN IN NEW SHOCK

by Our Showbiz Staff **Alison Tossoff**

LESLIE GRANTHAM has denied bringing the BBC into disrepute by taking part in a sick broadcast called *EastEnders*.

"Images featuring Grantham and others have been beamed into unsuspecting viewers homes via a device known as their television," claimed one Sunday tabloid. "These sick transmissions regularly feature storylines involving murders, rapes and incest, despite the fact that at that time of the evening children could be in the room."

"It is wrong that Grantham and his like can expose their lack of acting ability with sick transmissions like this that are being funded by us through the licence fee," said one horrified viewer.

Grantham however, quickly denied that he was involved. "I had nothing to do with it, I was too busy playing with myself on the internet to get involved with degrading filth like *EastEnders*."

Late News

CELEBRITY PARENTS GIVE CHILD SENSIBLE NAME SHOCK

THE showbiz world was rocked today when a celebrity couple named their baby something sensible.

"I'm sorry, but we just like the name Christopher," said the rock star and his actress girlfriend, "it was my grandfather's name."

"I can't understand why anyone would foister a weird name like Christopher on a child," said the teenage daughter of another rock star, Kiwi-Fruit Moonbeam Liquorice Banana Kangaroo Smith.

EASTENDERS SCRIPT EDITOR

LEAVE IT IN — LEAVE IT OUT

THOSE 'DIRTY'S IN FULL

Dirty Den Seedy TV actor caught by newspapers in pornography scandal

Dirty Des Seedy pornographer caught acting as newspaper proprietor

Dirty Digger Seedy newspaper and TV proprietor caught acting as if he was the Prime Minister

Dirty Harry Neither seedy nor pornographic but on TV constantly anyway

Dirty Wooster Little-known P.G. Wodehouse hero caught in a compromising position with Aunt Agatha *(That's enough. Ed.)*

THE WEEK IN PICTURES
Entente Cordiale

Not that 'cordiale', matey

Do you like frog's legs?

It's his hands I object to

BONJOUR!

"Bloody Brits!"

BLAIR – 'WE WILL HAND OVER SOVEREIGNTY'

by Our Political Correspondent **Hugh Rowe-Skeptic**

THE Prime Minister gave a categorical assurance last night that he would hand over the sovereignty of Great Britain to Brussels "at the first possible opportunity".

There have been fears that Britain would continue to hang on to the control of key British institutions, but Mr Blair was keen to reassure sceptics that this was not the case.

"All the vital areas have already been ceded to Brussels," he told reporters. "Parliament, the Law, the Police, Industry, Agriculture, Health and Safety and the shape of cucumbers are now effectively in the hands of non-local people.

"We may have to maintain a military presence in Britain," he continued, "but rest assured that it will be under the complete control of the European union.

"By the end of the year," he concluded, "we should pull out of Britain altogether."

AN EYE EXCLUSIVE
WE NAIL THOSE EUROSCEPTIC MYTHS ABOUT THE NEW CONSTITUTION

1 Under the new constitution, all red buses will be painted white and forced to drive on the right-hand side of the road. Untrue. The *Eye* says red buses will continue to be red and will come in threes, as per normal.

2 Under the new constitution, Britain's fishermen will have to re-train as supermarket check-out operatives in the enlarged European community. Untrue. The *Eye* says Britain's fishermen will merely be made redundant like anyone else.

3 Under the new constitution, the national anthem will be replaced by Edith Piaf's *"Je Ne Regrette Rien"*. Untrue. The *Eye* says the national anthem will remain *"Football's Coming Home"* as before. The new European anthem will be one verse each of *"The Marsellaise"* and *"Deutschland Uber Alles"*.

4 Under the new constitution, the Royal Family will be abolished and replaced by an EU President elected on a Big Brother voting system. Most likely candidates include Johnny Hallyday, Michael Schumacher and porn star La Mussolina. Untrue. The *Eye* says Britain's Royal Family will continue to be our leading tourist attraction and source of traditional humour.

5 Under the new constitution, English football players will be forced to play for Spanish clubs while the England manager will be a Swede. All London football clubs will be owned and run by foreigners and full of continental players. True. The *Eye* says "Er..."

Europe – The Choice Is Ours

Mr Blair's decision... historic importance... heart of Europe... little Englanders... left behind on sidelines... going forward... loss of sovereignty... straight bananas... traditional ambivalence... Atlantic ties... constitutional red lines... time to make a choice... yes... no... zzzzzz.
© *All newspapers.*

NEW EUROPEAN AGREEMENT

Let's shaft him!

It's a deal

LE PORN FLIES IN
– Angry Scenes At Racist Rally

by Our Political Correspondent **Hitler Hastings**

ONE OF Europe's most outrageous right-wingers, Jean Desmond Le Porn, flew into Canary Wharf today amid tight security to deliver an astonishing tirade of racist abuse against a number of shocked Telegraph executives.

Speaking in broken English, Le Porn claimed that the Telegraph was full of 'F***ing' Nazi-lovers and 'sh*tty' Hitler clones who wanted the Germans to take over the world.

Le Porn proceeded to goosestep around the office in the manner of Basil Fawlty, shouting "Don't mention the circulation war".

Deedes Day

He then told his burly henchmen to sing the nationalist anthem *'Desmond Über Alles'*.

One of them, a trembling Heinrich Haslum, obliged in a warbling falsetto.

But this was still not enough for Le Porn who pulled out a Luger pistol and threatened to kill Jeremy "Jerry" Deedes and his venerable

Le Porn

father Wilhelm von Deedes on the spot.

Asked about Le Porn's presence in Britain, the Home Secretary David Blunkett said, "We cannot stop Le Porn spreading his message of hate because he gave us £100,000 and is a friend of Tony Blair."

Would you like to have been at the meeting with Monsieur Le Porn? If so, you can read a full transcript of it on www.meinfilth@conservative.uk

CRIPES! YIKES! YIPPEE!

NEW CULTURE MONITOR BORIS

I KNOW ALL ABOUT THE ARTS, READER

IT'S NEXT TO THE ELBOW!

LORD BLACK and his Chums

Hello chums? Where's everyone gone?

Won't anyone talk to me?

Yes. You're nicked!

AMIEL THE PERIEL

I WANT MORE PAIRS OF SHOES!

HOW ABOUT THE BOOT?

P45

WILD SCENES AS EUROPE UNITES IN CELEBRATION

by Phil Space

OVER 400 billion 'New Europeans' came out onto the streets yesterday to celebrate the most important day in the history of the world.

After 40 centuries of bloodshed, war and torture, as the clocks struck midnight on 1 May 2004, Europe declared itself at last as one big happy family, reunited in a tidal wave of mutual love and boredom *(Surely 'willing cooperation'? Ed.).*

How They Celebrated – The Eye Takes A Panoramic View Of The 100 New Countries That Now Make Up The United States Of Europe

IN USTINOV, the capital of **Kovonia** (pop. 7302), colourfully dressed folk dancers joined together in the *Kornakova* to express their joy at Europe's day of destiny.

IN THE mountains of **Euthanasia** (pop. 3), colourfully dressed folk dancers celebrated their entry by eating platefuls of their traditional national cheese, *rumpelstiltskin*, which they are confident will soon become the favourite dish on Europe's breakfast tables.

COLOURFULLY dressed folk dancers from the forests of **Tesconia** (pop. 300 million) flocked into the central square of their capital Azda to toast "the new era of political and economic cooperation" in flagons of *shrek*, a highly alcoholic brandy-type drink distilled from cabbages.

IN **Great Britain,** millions of people colourfully dressed in their traditional national costume (jeans, t-shirts, trainers) turned on their televisions to see that the BBC was broadcasting round-the-clock folk-dancing to celebrate Europe's new dawn instead of the final of the Embassy Snooker *(cont. p. 94)*

(cont. p. 94)

● How did you celebrate on 1 May? If you would like to join the great Euro Festival, visit us now at www.zzzzz.co.eu

---

TV ROYAL MAIL PROGRAMME SHOCKS NATION

by Our Postal Staff **Phil Sack**

MILLIONS of viewers were stunned yesterday by a television programme which depicted the unbelievable truth about Britain's postal system.

The TV show followed one postman, referred to only as Pat, who was seen going about his business in Greendale, accompanied by a black and white cat. Pat was shown putting letters in his sack and then delivering them to the correct addresses.

Said one stunned viewer, "I couldn't believe my eyes! At no stage did he open the letters, steal the credit cards, or dump undelivered mail in a skip".

The Royal Mail was, however, quick to defend its staff. "Pat is just one isolated case. The public can rest assured that the vast majority of Britain's postmen are either useless or in league with Nigerian crime syndicates."

"I regret, señor, no last cigarette. This is our workplace."

Russell

400 YEARS OF BBC2

WHAT YOU MISSED IF YOU CAME IN HALFWAY THROUGH

Voiceover: ... and then of course there was the most epoch-making of all BBC2's epoch-making dramas, *Our Boys In The Northstuff*, by Alan Blackdale

(Shot of unemployed actors playing dominoes in North Country pub)

First Actor: 'appen I've got job wi' BBC2.

Second Actor: Jammy booger.

First Actor: It's t'roobish, but it pays t'rent.

Second Actor: I blame Thatcher.

Third Actor: Fooking bitch.

(Cut to lugubrious man in polo-neck sweater)

Alan Blackbeard *(for it is he)*: When I first submitted the script to the Controller of BBC2, he said "Alan, it just won't do. It's too brave, too brilliant, too powerful. I can't possibly show it."

(Cut to man in leather jacket, formerly Controller of BBC2)

Alain de Botney *(for it is he)*: When I first saw the script of 'Northstuff', I knew at once I had to have it. It was so brave, so briliant, so powerful.

Voiceover: And the rest of course was TV history. But no year could match 1982, the year when the legendary *Toast Programme* marked an epoch-making watershed in BBC2's documentary output.

(Cut to balding, middle-aged man in polo-neck sweater. Caption: 'Michael Hovis, presenter of The Toast Programme 1982-1994')

Hovis *(for it is he)*: It seems incredible now that, in those days, and I'm talking about the early '80s, no one had ever thought of making a programme devoted to toast. Particularly when you think that toast plays such an important part in all our lives, on a daily basis.

(Cut to blonde woman standing in

kitchen with a younger Hovis, holding up a piece of toast. Caption: 'Sandra Sunblest, co-presenter The Toast Programme, 1982-1998')

Sunblest *(for it is she)*: Go on, Mike, try it!

Hovis: M-m-m-m, that's surprisingly good!

Sunblest: And you'll like it even more when I put some of this Marmite on it!

Hovis: Marmite? You must be joking, Sandra! This is what young people are eating today – fishpaste!

Voiceover: And talking of young people, it wasn't long before BBC2 discovered the need for an epoch-making show catering specifically for the long-overlooked teenage audience.

(Cut to tall woman with green hair and protruding teeth)

Janet Street-Yentob *(for it is she)*: All you could see on telly in those days was old people doing old people's things, like making toast, and it was so b-o-o-ring!

(Cut to gyrating group of young persons wearing silver foil miniskirts filmed at crazy camera angles, with text running over the top reading 'Coming up soon – more captions you can't read'. Cut to middle-aged black man in lurex jump suit. Caption: 'Rimsky Normaskoff, presenter of Rubbish!!! 1984-1985')

Normaskoff *(for it is he)*: Basically, it was really epoch-making to get young people

on screen doing things for themselves, and not just sitting around making toast. *Rubbish!!!* was the show that stretched the envelope. It was BBC2 at its bravest, its most brilliant, its most powerful.

Voiceover: And talking of epoch-making television, who can ever forget the late-night arts programme which re-defined the whole nature of late-night arts programmes. In the words of its first producer, *The Late Nights Arts Programme* was "as brave, as brilliant and as powerful as it was epoch-making".

(Cut to old footage of woman with frizzy hair and red-rimmed glasses)

Sarah Doonatwatch *(for it is she)*: Tonight on *The Late Night Arts Programme* we've got the German artist, Hans Pumpernickel, who makes sculptures out of toast. Then we shall be looking at Episode 734 of *Our Boys Up The Northstuff*, the searing new BBC drama, and a new book about Britain's youth culture by Rimsky Normaskoff. But first our guest critics.

(We see footage of two men in polo-neck sweaters having a fight)

Voiceover: But if there was one programme which summed up the epoch-making contribution of BBC2 more than any other, it must surely be the most popular programme the channel has ever put out in all of its 40 years, *The Boys From The Pot Black Stuff*.

(Shot of snooker ball disappearing down side pocket)

Bald Man In Bow Tie: Booger.

2nd Bald Man In Bow Tie: I blame Thatcher.

Ends

Have you got a favourite memory of BBC2? Join the big BBC2 debate on our website *www.boysfromtheblackslap.co.uk*

KEVIN SPACEY IN EARLY MORNING WALK IN PARK SHOCK

Well, mugger me!

BEARD & HAIR GEL

Hands up those in favour of ignoring the Geneva Convention

'THIS TORTURE MUST STOP'

Blair's plea

by Our Political Staff
Lunchtime O'Buse

THE PRIME Minister made a dramatic call to the nation last night to stop torturing him with suggestions that he knew about human rights abuses in Iraq.

"I have been subjected to brutal interrogations," said the Prime Minister, "with people trying to get me to break down and admit my war crimes."

Electric shock and awe

"On one occasion," he claimed, "I was taken from my home late at night and bright lights were shone in my face. Then they started filming me, and at one point I was humiliated by my jacket being removed."

He continued: "One of them, I think he was called Jeremy, kept on and on asking me the same question – 'You knew all about this didn't you?'

"In the end I just wanted it to stop. I would have said anything, even 'sorry', which I did but I don't mean it."

ON OTHER PAGES: Why I have changed my mind about Iraq by Johann Hari-Kiri, Minette Marinade, Tony Parshole and everybody else except Melanie Phillips **pp2-94**

TORTURE SHOCK

I was only giving orders

That Fatty Soames Defence of the Army in full

IN ANY organisation there are bound to be a few rotten apples but I know the British Army and I have absolute confidence that the military authorities will act swiftly and justly to stamp out these rotten apples, although they haven't so far... er... I know the British Army well and I am certain that what we are dealing with here is a small number of bad eggs of the type one wouldn't eat in an omelette however delicious... er... our troops are the finest in the world and unlike the Americans we have had long experience in Northern Ireland of doing this sort of thing and then holding enquiries about it... er... and it's clearly just a few rotten tomatoes in the soup with croutons and some parmesan please and then I'll have the saddle of lamb washed down with a couple of rotten bottles of... er... where was I? I know the British Army extremely well having served for over three luncheons... er... and all I can say that these disclosures make life very difficult for the chaps in the restaurant and of course the field. If these Iraqis get the idea into their heads that we are torturing them, then they are going to get pretty shirty and before long they'll be trying not to get captured in case they get murdered... so I suggest that we all shut up about this and go and have our lunch at once, otherwise we may not get a table, it fills very quickly at this time of year..."

Boris Johnson on his doubts surrounding the conduct of the Iraqi war

Golly! Cripes! What's going on? When I signed up to support this war lark, no one said it was going to turn nasty!

Makes you feel a bit of a chump! I mean, didn't we go over there to liberate Johnny Iraqi? You know – crowds cheering, flags waving, happy smiling kiddies chewing gum, that sort of thing?

Nobody mentioned torture. Chaps getting their private parts kicked in. That's a bit strong, isn't it? We didn't even do that sort of thing at Eton. Well, we did actually, but that's not the point.

The point is that old Boris has been sold a pup by our Yankee cousins, and I'm feeling a bit of a prat. Blimey!

● **Do you think the new Shadow Minister for the Arts is a bit of a chump? Join the 'Big Chump Debate' at ww.beanoboris.com**

VILE

BUT IS <u>THIS</u> PICTURE A FAKE?

THIS picture has shocked the entire civilised world.

It shows the whole newspaper industry pissing all over Daily Mirror editor Piers Moron for publishing some dodgy photographs in his paper.

The Eye says: **This humiliating abuse is illegal and should be stopped immediately! Leave Piers alone!** *(Surely some mistake? Ed.)*

This appears to be a picture of Piers Moron working in his office. But is it? Moron experts last night pointed out a host of discrepancies which indicate that the newspaper was clearly a fake:

1. The clock on the wall shows the time at 2pm. Insiders point out that Moron would never be back from lunch until 5.30pm.

2. Moron does not display any signs of the savage beating he recently received at the hands of TV motoring expert Jeremy Clarkson.

3. There is no photo on the desk of gorgeous, pouting Marina Hyde.

4. Also absent from the desk is Moron's prized 'Viglen' mouse-mat, a souvenir of his historic 'share tipping' triumph.

5. Further clinching evidence that the desk in the picture cannot be genuine is that it contains no half-empty bottles.

6. Moron's shoelaces appear to be neatly tied. Staffers insist that he has never learned how to perform this simple task.

But last night an unrepentant Moron hit back at his critics. "Of course I am a fake. The idea that I am the editor of a national newspaper is patently absurd."

"This is neither the time nor the place to release your endorphins, George"

MARY ANN BIGHEAD
WHAT I DID ON MY HOLIDAYS

THIS bank holiday I took my daughter on a weekend break to Auschwitz.

This was a good idea because she is so clever and so am I. We both understood everything, unlike the other people who were there who were not nearly as clever as me and my daughter.

Some people think that Auschwitz is too awful an experience for a child, but luckily my daughter is incredibly mature and imaginative and talkative and bright and actually very much like her mother.

Some other people also brought their children to Auschwitz, but they had ordinary children and I told these parents off for their stupidity. My daughter, however, fully understood the implications of our visit, ie that I would have to turn our intensely personal private journey into a few hundred words to fill up my column in the Times. Luckily, I am so clever that I do not notice anything odd about this.

Our pilgrimage has, however, reminded us of the real message of these appalling places – that I am very clever and so is my daughter.

© Mary Ann Bighead

MICHAEL HOWARD
Curriculum Vitae

1666:
Born Transylvania. Son of a humble count, Vlad Dracul.

1669:
Attends Transylvania Grammar School where he gains an A grade in Human Physiology.

1702-1897:
Terrorises local villagers and appears in films pursued by Dr Van Helsing.

1983:
Elected MP for Folkstone and Hythe.

1987:
Introduces Stake Tax and outlaws the carrying of crucifixes in public places.

1993:
Becomes Home Secretary and bans garlic.

1997:
Attempted exorcism by Dr Ann Widdecombe fails and Howard retreats to coffin in house of commons crypt.

2003:
Awakens to become leader of the Conservative Party.

2004:
Becomes more popular than Tony Blair, thus provoking this pathetic advert in an attempt to scare off voters during the local elections.

Britain is working. Don't let The Tories drink your blood and make you join the Undead.

Labour
www.labour.org.uk

THE VOICE OF THE SEXPRESS

TONY BLAIR has lost the cheque *(Surely "trust"? Ed.)* of the *Daily Sexpress*. The Prime Minister has let us down. As proprietor, I even went to tea with him. But nothing has changed. There is still violent crime on our streets; public services are still in decline; immigration has still not been tackled. And I am still regarded as a seedy figure of fun. We all hoped that it would be different under New Labour. We all hoped that Europe would be sorted out, that taxes would be lowered and that I would become a respectable figure who could bid for the *Daily Telegraph*.

Yet what happened? Iraq is a mess, council tax is rising, public transport is failing and I remain a sleazy pornographer on the make.

That is why the *Sexpress* is switching its alliance to the Tory Party. And so are all my other titles.

Mr Blair, from now on you no longer enjoy the backing of *Asian Babes, Grannies on the Job* and *Big Black and Bouncy*. Their editors, like Peter Hill of the *Sexpress*, have all independently decided to do what they are told and support Michael Howard. From now on, it is not New Labour, but the Conservatives who are the party for right-handed wankers *(Surely "right-thinking readers"? Ed.)*.

**Sir Dirtswell Desmond,
245 Blackteens Road,
London SE X**

Radio 4
What You Missed

Jim Naughtie *(for it is he)*: These pictures of Diana, Princess of Wales, in her dying agony, which have been shown on American television – I mean, would you say that they were disgusting, tasteless, repugnant and offensive, and should never have been broadcast?

Royal Expert: Well, we have seen these pictures before, and they were very indistinct, and they were only on the screen for a few seconds...

Naughtie: So what you're saying is that a lot of people would have been really outraged by this intrusion into private grief? I mean, what if the Princes were to see these pictures of their mother dying? Isn't that stepping way beyond the bounds of any normal standards of decency?

Royal Expert: Well, you know, I wouldn't personally...

Naughtie: ... just how long is this media obsession with the late Princess Diana going to last? Are we going to have an endless succession of programmes picking over every detail of her death in a rather ghoulish way? Are we ever going to talk about anything else?

Royal Expert: It seems not.

Naughtie: Well, that's all we've got time for. But after the news we'll be going over live to America, to talk to some of the people who watched those horrific and shocking pictures, and they'll be telling us just how offensive and disgusting they found them, and hopefully filling in a few details about blood and so on. And now, *Thought For The Day*, with Abu Hamza, the Chief Imam of the Finsbury Park Mosque.

Hamza: You know, in a very real sense, we should kill all the Jews and then blow up everyone in the West for *(Cont. 94 kHz)*

"I told you the DVD player needed attention"

POLAND'S PRESIDENT FLIES IN

He says he can do the plumbing while he's here

Lines Written On The Dismissal Of Mr Piers Moron From The Editorship Of The Daily Mirror BY WILLIAM REES-MCGONAGALL

'Twas in the year two thousand and four
That Mr Piers Morgan was ignominiously shown the door.
Said the managing director of Trinity Mirror, Miss Sly Bailey,
"You are no longer fit to be the editor of a famous national daily."

The staff of the *Daily Mirror* had never enjoyed such a treat
As the sight of Mr Moron being frogmarched into the street.
He was not even given time to clear his desk,
His crime being considered so grotesque.

On the *Mirror*'s top floor, the bosses had had enough.
"For too long we have allowed you to get away with this appalling stuff."
They then read out a list of his past misdemeanours.
"Thanks to you, our great newspaper has been taken to the cleaners."

One thing which particularly enraged the men in suits
Was the sharetipping scandal which gave Moron the chance to fill his boots.
Readers may recall this murky affair
When the *Mirrror* told readers to buy a particular share.
The name of the company concerned was Viglen –
"It will rise as high," said the City Slickers, "as the tower of Big Ben."

Only then did it emerge that Moron himself, no less,
Had invested heavily in the shares before his paper went to press.
No sooner had his readers rushed to follow suit
Than Moron sold out, thus doubling his loot.

For a long time in this vein I could continue to bore on.
About the financial shenanigans of Mr Piers Moron.
Of course I have no desire to mention his "bit on the side"
(Whose name, incidentally, was Miss Marina Hyde).

Thus ended in ignominy his far from glittering career
Over which very few of my readers will be inclined to shed a tear.
The offence for which Mr Moron was given the sack
Was even more heinous than that committed by Lord Black.

By publishing pictures of an alleged act of torture
In place of the customary headline "Phew! What A Scorcher!"
It was clear to all the nation that Moron's pictures were faked
And his defence for publishing them was blatantly half-baked.

"Our photos showed events of the type that might have taken place,"
Said Moron, in a bid to save himself from complete disgrace.
But even for all this he might not have been shown the door
If the sales of the Mirror had not been falling through the floor.

His faked photographs and collapsing circulation
Combined to inflict on him a terrible humiliation.
But perhaps this sad figure will somehow manage to survive
As the host of a soft-porn chat show on Channel Five.

Daily Mail

60 Page Special

40 pence

FOR BUSH AND EMPIRE

Friday 21 MARCH 2003

ALLIES ADVANCE –

'WEAPONS SURE TO BE FOUND SOON'

Premier's Historic Pledge

by W.M. Deedes

THE Prime Minister, the Rt. Hon. Winstony Blair, last night appeared on the balcony of Buckingham Palace to announce to cheering crowds (Sid and Doris Mandelson) that British troops, side by co-side with our American allies, are now advancing into Iraq on all fronts.

"Our boys are definitely on the verge of a major breakthrough in finding the enemy's secret weapons of mass destruction which are pointing directly at the heart of London and are ready to be launched within 45 years," said the Prime Minister.

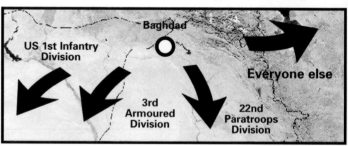

Desert of the type Allied troops are reported to be advancing across

BAGHDAD OR BUST

THAT was the message from thousands of smiling Tommies as they drove over the border to Basra, to be greeted by delighted locals with showers of explosives and happy cries of "death to the infidel".

STATUE 'DEFINITELY DEAD'

by Our Special Correspondent
HUGH VERY-ROPEY

AS the first Allied correspondent to reach the heart of Iraq, I saw with my own eyes the scene where only a few hours before the hated dictator had been toppled from his plinth. There could be no doubt about it, the hated statue was dead, his reign of terror finally at an end.

HOW SADDAM WAS FOOLED

BY A brilliant masterstroke of counter-intelligence, Saddam was fooled into thinking that the Allied invasion would never come.

Night after night, President Bush had appeared on television, announcing that the Anglo-American invasion of Iraq could take place "at any time".

Saddam, believing Bush to be an idiot, ignored the warnings, assuming that Bush was having him on, and that America's real intention was to invade somewhere else, such as North Korea.

Reuters

How The Allies Will Escape From Iraq

Baghdad

US 1st Infantry Division

Everyone else

3rd Armoured Division

22nd Paratroops Division

Just Fancy That!

Did crossword compiler Archimedes of the Daily Telegraph give away vital clues which could have tipped off Saddam Hussein over the allies' top secret plans to invade his country?

Last Tuesday's 9 down, "A bra's confused in Iraq", gave the answer "Basra" – a clear hint to the Iraqi dictator as to where allied troops were heading for.

Another clue, 11 across, accurately

predicted what would happen to Iraq after the allies had taken over the country.

The answer "total shambles" so worried Anglo-American intelligence chiefs that they seriously considered calling the whole invasion off.

PIGEONS WILL FIND BIN LADEN

THE BBC last night revealed that teams of highly-trained pigeons are being dropped behind enemy lines, in order to sniff out the world's most hated man, Osama bin Liner.

"The government is confident that the Pigeon Force will root out Al Qaeda and destroy it for ever," said a War Office spokesman.

"It will come in handy, Corporal, if they drop those weapons of mass destruction on us!"

WILL INVASION AFFECT HOUSE PRICES?

THERE was concern last night at the Treasury at the prospect of the Allied invasion causing a fall in house prices, leading to a collapse in morale on the home front (cont. p. 94)

D-DAY IN PICTURES

Lest we forget…

…I've got an election in November

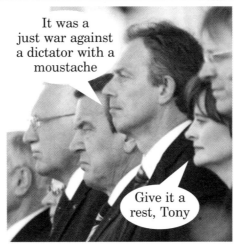

It was a just war against a dictator with a moustache

Give it a rest, Tony

We're allies at last…

…against America!

PRINCE CHARLES' MEDALS

IN RESPONSE to readers asking about the medals Prince Charles was wearing during the D-Day celebrations, Private Eye gives a quick at-a-glance guide to our most decorated heir to the throne.

■ **The Grand Order of the Carbuncle.**
For his part in the campaign against modern architecture.

■ **The Imperial Cross of Asparagus.**
For his brave stand against artificial GM fertilisers.

■ **The Queen Victoria Iron Cross for Watercolours.**
Awarded for "Donkey in the Moonlight" 1982.

■ **The King Edward VII Star for Adultery** *(surely Gallantry, Ed?)*
For his services at the Battle of Camilla-Legover (1984-2004).

(That's enough medals, Ed.)

GLENDA SLAGG

FLEET STREET'S MISTRESS ROYAL!!?!

■ **QUEEN CAMILLA** – pull the other one, mister, it's got wedding bells on it!?! Or rather it hasn't!???! Let's face it, you'll never be our Queen of Hearts because you look like the back end of a bus!!!? – No disrespect, Ma'am!!! If Charles has any sense, he'll keep you out of sight in a horsebox where you belong!!?!? No disrespect again, Ma'am, but kids today want their queen to look like Posh Spice or Jordan – not Lily Savage on a bad hair day!!?!? Or Bad *Heir* day???!! Geddit??????!

■ FOR God's sake, Charles, make an honest woman of her!!??! The whole nation has warmed to this lovable Queen of Hearts who likes a fag and a drink just like the rest of us!!?! If you don't marry her, you must be barmy (no disrespect, sire), so get down on your royal bended knee and pop the question: "Camilla, will you help me up again?" (Glenda's little joke!!!) But seriously, Chazza, hurry up and get her to the church on time, ie before you die??!?!?

■ **GORDON RAMSAY** – aren'tcha-sickofhim? This foul-mouthed Chef leaves a nasty taste in your mouth – just like his food!!??! Know what I'd like, Gordon???! I'd like to microwave you goodbye for ever?!? F*** off, Gordon!!??! And I don't mean flambé!!?? Geddit????!

■ GORDON RAMSAY – What a Michelin Star!!?!!! With his chef's hat and his fruity language, he makes cooking f**!!!? That's Fun, mister, with a capital F!!!?? It's the best television I've seen since the last programme he was on??!?!? Mmmmm!!!!! Delicious!???! Pass me the f***ing pan, Gordon, and I'll f** up an egg!!??!

■ **SEBASTIAN COE** – What a disgrace!!??! How can he be our Mr Olympics when he's running around with his trousers round his ankles??!? No wonder London's gonna lose the Olympics when its star performer is hoping to beat the world record for the four-minute bonk!!?? On your marks, get set… go away!!?!

■ SO Lord Coe had a bit of nookie on the side – so what???? This is the twentieth century for gawd's sake!!!!?? *(No, it isn't. Ed.)* Surely we're grown up enough not to care whether this super athlete has spent his time a-rumpin' and a-pumpin' with every gorgeous gal he meets instead of flying the flag for his country!!??! What's the matter with us????! Let's face it, London is the sex capital of the world and our Seb is just the man to have on the job!!?! Geddit???!??

■ HERE THEY ARE – Glenda's Super-Thursday-Men (Geddit!!?)

● **Robert Kilroy-Silk** – UKIP's Mr Sex!!?! U can come round and KIP at my place anytime, big boy!!?!

● **Jose Mourinho** – You're Chelsea's Mr Big!!??! Well, come and prove it by scoring with this gal!!???!

● **The Dalai Lama** – Crazy name, crazy guy!!!?!?

Byeeee!!!

THE DAILY TELEGRAPH
Friday, June 11, 2004

Letters *to the Editor*

SIR – The whole nation will have been outraged by press reports that the captain of the England cricket team, a Mr Vaughan, was given permission to leave the field of play in the event of his lady wife giving birth during the match. No doubt the cause of this absurd ruling lies with our friends in Brussels, which is yet another reason for supporting the UK Independence Party. I well recall a match in India between the Maharajah of Napaul's XI and a team representing the local business community, the Boxwallahs. When the captain of the Boxwallahs, a Mr Vijay Hatterjee-Singh, was at the crease, on 36 not out, news was brought to him that his house was on fire, his cow had fallen into the Ganges and his wife had been set upon by a band of marauding muggers. As the umpire, I very properly ruled that he should not be allowed to leave the field until he had completed his innings, in accordance with Law 42.6(c) laid down by the game's governing body, the Marylebone Cricket Club. To his great credit, Hatterjee-Singh remained at the wicket and went on to score an unbeaten 378. He fully deserved the excellent turnout at his wife's funeral the next day, but alas his cow was never seen again. One cannot envisage the henpecked Mr Vaughan displaying such admirable stoicism in the face of adversity!

Sir H. Gussett
Dunbowlin, Trescothick, Cornwall

MONASTERY OF DREAMS

by SYLVIE KRIN, author of *'Heir of Sorrows'*, *'La Dame Aux Camillas'* and *'Never Too Old'*

THE STORY SO FAR: Seeking peace, solitude and spiritual illumination, Charles makes a pilgrimage to the remote Greek monastery on Mount Bathos. Now read on...

CHARLES climbed the last of the seven thousand, four hundred and eighty-four steps cut into the rock face, which for centuries had led pilgrims up from the sandy shore to the holiest spot in the Greek world.

Behind him struggled a procession of aged monks carrying the Prince's few simple possessions – his special herbal double bed, his water-colour painting equipment, his forty suitcases full of freshly-pressed Fry & Laurie shirts, a selection of his favourite talking plants and his beloved polo pony, Mummy's Boy.

At the top of the steps, standing in the monastery's tiny courtyard, looking down to the wine-dark Aegean thousands of feet below, was the venerable, black-cloaked figure of the abbot, Father Stassinopoulos.

"Welcome to Mount Bathos, sir," said the bearded holy man. "Truly God has sent you here, whoever you are."

"Er, Kalamari," Charles mumbled, searching hurriedly through his phrase book for an appropriate greeting, "er, retsina, para kalo."

The old man smiled sympathetically, as he led Charles through a gloomy passageway to his tiny cell, with its window looking out on the gaily-painted fishing boats dotting the distant sea.

"I will leave you alone now to enjoy the silence," said the abbot. "We eat bread and water at half-past three in the morning, which is our main meal of the day, and then we pray the rest of the day until we go to bed at 5 in the evening. You will soon get used to our simple ways..."

SIMPLE ways. That was what Charles had been craving for so long. And here at last on Mount Bathos he felt he had come to the very heart of what the inner-search thingie was all about.

No phones. No television. No journalists hanging around. And, best of all, no women!

Of course, Camilla was a very good egg, in all sorts of ways. And his mother, the Queen, she had her good points, game old thing, and all that.

But goodness me, these monks really had the right idea.

Time to oneself, without some woman breathing cigarette smoke over one's organic honey-flakes at breakfast, and asking silly questions like "Do you really have to wear a Guards tie with your pyjamas?" or "When are we going to get married, Chazza?"

As he heard the distant chanting of the monks in their chapel hewn from the living rock, he thought of all the sacred wisdom which had been accumulating in this holy place for two thousand years.

What was it his friend and mentor Sir Laurens van der Post had told him, when they were visiting the site of the ancient oracle on the island of Paxos? "It's all Greek to me"? No, that wasn't it.

"Never on Sunday"? No, that wasn't it either.

It would come to him later...

I WILL come to you later," the old monk had said. And now here he was, his grizzled beard glinting in the candlelight, ready to show him the greatest treasures the monks had accumulated over the millennia.

Charles followed him through the labyrinth of narrow passages, as the monk's sandals slapped on the polished stone slabs ahead of him.

Stronger and stronger grew the smell of incense as they approached the tiny door of the "Holy of Holies".

Charles's heart began to thump faster. This was incredible, he thought. Here he was at the very heart of this whole Orthodox thingie, the faith of his Greek ancestors, going back through his father all the way to... was it Agamemnon, who he'd seen in that new film Camilla had dragged him to in Cirencester...

"... And here you see the very precious icon of Agios Nikolaos."

The abbot held up a flickering candle to illuminate the cracked surface of the 6th-Century masterpiece.

"And here we have another very sacred icon showing Agios Giorgios, or Saint George as you call him."

"Oh, yes," enthused Charles. "He comes from my country, Saint George of England."

The old monk looked puzzled, but then, his face lighting up, he moved on round the corner. "And here you see the greatest jewel in all our collection!"

Charles was momentarily blinded by the hundreds of candles burning in the incense-laden air at the foot of the largest icon of all.

"Very holy woman, many miracles," murmured the abbot reverently, "greatest lady who ever lived."

As the elderly monk prostrated himself on the floor, Charles's eyes became accustomed to the half-light.

No, oh no, it couldn't be. Surely not!

But the face looking down on him with an expression of serene contempt was unmistakable.

"Yes," whispered Father Stassinopoulos, "it is Agia Diana, Saint Diana."

At that moment, an Aegean breeze wafted down the passageway, extinguishing the candles in a sudden gust.

Charles stood alone in the darkness. It really was, what was the word? Appalling...

That Cork University Honorary Degree In Full

SALUTAMUS PIERCUS BROSNANICUS, ACTORUM HIBERNICUM POPULARUM CINEMATOGRAPHICUM. NOTABILE IN FILMUS ESPIONAGUS THRILLARICUM 'NOMEN EST BONDUS, JACOBUS BONDUS'. CELEBRATUS AGENTUS BRITANNICUS, CODEX OOVII, LICENSUS ASSASSINATUS. IN SUCCESSIONE SEANUS CONNERENSIS, GEORGIUS LAZENBENSIS, ROGERUS MORONICUS, SEANUS CONNERENSIS BIS, ET TIMOTHEUS DALTONICUS. VOCE POPULARE DICET 'PIERCUS BENE EST, SED NON BENE QUAM SEAN CONNERENSIS'. EXAMPLO 'MEDICUS NON', 'DIGITUS AUREUS' ET 'SEMPER DIAMONDES' (SATIS EST – EDITUS).

© The University of Cork (formerly Flannegan Bar and Post Office – bang on door and ask for Seamus).

Daily Mail, Friday, May 14, 2004

Time Someone Stuck Up For Rain!

Says **Max Hastings**, The World's Worst Columnist

THIS morning I awoke to the familiar drumming sound of raindrops on my window pane.

"Oh dear, it's raining again!" Already I could hear the long-faced Jeremiahs bemoaning what, for some of us at least, is the most uplifting sound the English countryside can offer.

I have never understood why it is fashionable to complain about a little drop of rain.

The barbecue brigade moan that it is spoiling their weekend fun, and that now they will have to stay huddled round their Aga with their sad jacket potatoes and burned bangers.

The white-flannelled fools rush for the pavilion, belly-aching that rain is going to "stop play".

So be it, say I! There's nothing like putting on your Barbour and your wellies, to go splashing through the puddles!

Splish, splash, splish, splash! Rommel, my favourite black labrador, just loves it, bounding across the rain-sodden meadows with a disembowelled fox between his jaws!

I know how he feels. Who are the fools who sing "Rain, rain, go to Spain"?

Why should the Spaniards have all the fun?

I say, "Rain, rain, stay here in England". And I'll tell you something else... Rain's got a job to do. Unlike myself, who just sits here, waiting for the Mail to ring up and ask me to fill up page 10.

© *Hitlertrash Productions (Hungerford)*

● Are you pro- or anti-rain? Join the "Great Rain Debate" at www.rainyawn.co.uk

---

Isn't it amazing the way the eyes seem to follow the Interns round the room?

'SWEET AND CRISP MANUFACTURERS TARGET CHILDREN' SHOCK

THE WORLD was said to be stunned by a shocking report just out, which claims that companies who make sweets and crisps deliberately target children when it comes to marketing their products.

On Other Pages

ELECTION 2004

How you won't vote on 10 June, because you can't be bothered

Voting paper for European, Local and Mayoral Elections, 10 June 2004
Neasden Central Ward of the South-East Euro-Region

(A) Statement by Elector
All voters must fill in this section.

I .... *(fill in name)* am the person to whom this voting paper was originally addressed, even though it had to be left with the lady at 81b across the road because, by the time the postman arrived, I was at work / down the social / claiming my benefit/in the pub.

(B) Witness Statement

I .... *(fill in name)*, the woman across the street, certify that the person named in the Statement by Elector is himself, or possibly his brother who looks very like him, it's uncanny. The voter has satisfied me as to his identity and has asked me over for a sherry to say thank you.

(C) Witness to the Witness

I .... *(fill in name)* was just walking down the street minding my own business when I was stopped by this couple asking me to witness their marriage or something of the sort, which I was duly happy to do although, strictly between ourselves, I think they'd been at the sherry.

(D) Health & Safety Disclaimer

Before proceeding to cast your vote, please complete the following declaration that you are (a) over 18; (b) not suffering from any contagious disease, such as Meningitis B, Hepatitis A, Vitamin C; (c) not intending to sue the Electoral Committee for any injury which may be sustained by filling in this form, e.g. tennis elbow, repetitive strain injury, death by boredom.

(E) The Act of Voting

You are now ready to move on to the solemn act of recording your vote(s) for the candidate(s) of your choice. IMPORTANT: Remember that you have only ONE vote, except in elections for the Greater London Assembly, where you have three (or is it the other way round?)

List of Candidates in full

Read carefully through this list of candidates, making sure that you do not confuse the names of individual candidates with those standing under the 'party list' system. If you have any problems understanding this, please do not hesitate to contact our Helpline via our call centre in Madras. Our trained staff will then instruct you in how to record your vote for Mrs Gandhi.

1	**British Union Of Democratic Fascists** 1. Conrad Blackshirt 2. A. Cabbie 3. Sir Oswald Mosley	
2	**No To GM Pro-Windfarm Party** 1. Lord Melchett 2. Sir Jonathan Porridge 3. Prince of Wales 4. Sally Green	
3	**Liberal Democrat Pro-Cycle Lanes And EU Constitution Party** 1. Simon Servile 2. Polly Technic 3. Ron Beard	
4	**Conservatives Putting Losing First And Saying Yes And No To Europe** 1. C. Dracula 2. O. Letslose 3. Beano Boris	
5	**The Saddam Hussein Respect The Moustache Alliance** 1. G. Galloway 2. P. Spart 3. K. Loon	
6	**Pisces** Do not attempt to fill in any forms today if you are a Piscean. It could have unforeseen consequences! You may be approached by a woman across the road asking for your help. Be generous with the sherry!	

7	**Labour Let's Pretend There Isn't An Election Going On Party** 1. Patsy Jacket 2. Suzi Anglepoise 3. Debbie Lampshade	
8	**FCUKIP** 1. R. Kilroy-Sacked 2. W. Really-Smugg 3. Dame Joan Harpie-Collins	FCUKIP
9	**INDEPENDENT** 1. Ted Nutter	

When you have completed the above form, fold it carefully along the line marked A-B and fold this again along the line B-C, making sure that no one sees you performing this secret action.

If they do, you will be liable on summary conviction to a fine of £500.

Then take the folded voting form, ensuring that the address of your regional returning officer is uppermost in the transparent window, and place the form carefully in the waste disposal receptacle provided for this purpose.

CONGRATULATIONS!!!!

You have now become the first person in Britain to complete the 2004 voting form. You have thus become eligible for a fabulous prize, which might be any of the following: 1) Electric toaster; 2) Midweek break in the Ramada Inn, Neasden; 3) A year's subscription to The Spectator.

RING NOW on our premium-rate line 09860-511-511 (£12 a second) to ascertain which of these prizes you haven't won.

If you do not complete this form (or indeed receive it) your vote will not be wasted. It will be counted as a vote for the Labour Party.

That Thatcher Eulogy For President Reagan In Full

WE CELEBRATE today the greatest statesman the world has ever known, a colossus who bestrode the globe and reshaped the destiny of the planet. Born of humble origins, this leader rose to the highest office of state by strength of character, uncompromising politics and an unswerving sense of right and wrong, personally bringing about the end of communism, and the revitalisation of the international economy. But enough of me. We are here to remember Ronald Reagan, who was privileged to have known the woman they called "The Iron Lady" *(cont. for 94 minutes)*.

© Charles Moore, the Daily Maggiegraph, Canary Cold Wharf.

BIG BROTHER
An Apology From Channel Four

AS THE makers of Big Brother, we would like to apologise for the violence and debauchery which has unfortunately marred recent episodes of this popular reality entertainment show.

When we commissioned the latest series, peopled it with specially chosen exhibitionists, retards and mentally unstable individuals and then provided them with copious amounts of alcohol, we had no idea that scenes of drunkenness, fighting and lewd behaviour would ensue.

We were rather hoping for something more extreme, such as a multiple murder followed by a cannibalistic orgy, culminating in a mass suicide – leading to record viewing figures for Channel Four.

Sadly, we will have to make do with the disappointing ratings of a mere seven million viewers.

© Mark Thomson, Head of Channel 4 and Director Elect of the BBC in cooperation with Enditall Productions.

POETRY CORNER

In Memoriam Ronald Reagan, 40th President of the United States of America (1911-2004)

So. Farewell
Then Ronald
Reagan

Famous film
Star and
President.

"One for
The Gipper",
Yes, that
Was your
Catchphrase.

Now you are
"One for the
Reaper".

E.J. Thribb (17½)

EDEXCEL

A-Level
2004
MATHEMATICS

1 If A has two hundred pounds to spend and B has five hundred pounds to spend, and this exam paper is on sale for twice as much as the chemistry paper, but only two thirds of the cost of the biology paper, how many more times will student B be interviewed by police investigating the theft than student A?

(Answer: Yours for £50 – see you round the back of the bike-sheds in 5 minutes)

My eBay

cherie boo (5)

Items I'm Bidding On (1-5 of 5 items)

	Current Price	Postage Cost	Bids
Brazilian Mother-Goddess Re-Birthing Crystals *genuine*			
	£2,500	£1.50	1
Shoe Trees (pack 300 pairs, nearly new)			
	£199.99	£49.99	1
CD: 'The Spinners – Greatest Hits'			
	£2.99	£1.00	1
'Con-Tea-Ki' Tea Co. Slimming Tea – pkt. 48 bags			
	£99.99	£1.00	1
'A to Z of Bristol' – good condition			
	£2.99	£1.00	1

Items I'm Selling (1-4 of 4 items)

	Current Price	Postage Cost	Bids
Handcrafted Scottish Wood, Child's Christening Mug (unwanted gift)			
	£0.99p	Free!	0
Men's Fitness Exercise Bike (used once)			
	£30.00	Buyer to collect	0
12-volume set 'History of Socialism', impressive binding, still in box			
	£2.99	£1.00	0
'Be Your Own PR Manager' 'Smile Your Way to Success!' 2 paperbacks, as new			
	£1.99	£1.00	0

WHO'S WHO IN THE PARTY THAT HAS SHAKEN BRITISH POLITICS TO ITS FOUNDATIONS

The 12 UKIP MEPs Who Have Pledged Themselves To 'Tear Down The EU Brick By Brick'

ASHLEY MOAT, South East, formerly chairman of Moat and Beam, the Surrey garden centre chain. Keen amateur bicyclist and Scrabble player.

NIGEL BORAGE, South East, former manager of the HSBC, Chorleywood. Longtime addict of the Daily Telegraph crossword.

BILL DAFT, South West, runs a futon-importing business, 'U-Kip Soundly', in Paignton. Once represented Devon in a local kayak racing competition.

HUGO TREMLETT, East Midlands, former hotelier from Skegness, now vice-chairman of the South Derbyshire Morris Dancing and Model Railway Club.

GERALD WHEEN, Eastern, former poultry keeper in Norfolk. Once played the ukelele in the Saxmundham All Stars Skiffle Group.

DAVID WAGSTAFFE, North West, formerly entertainments officer of the Morecambe Marinerama and Aqualeisure Centre. Could be Foreign Secretary in a UKIP government.

MONTY PRATTWINKLE, West Midlands, retired whisky salesman for the Glen McHackey Distillery Co. Keen amateur golfer (handicap 48).

(That's enough UKIP superstars. Ed.)

"Yes, well, thank you Councillor for the danger to birdlife demonstration"

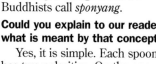

BORESDAY

Cut-Out-And-Throw-Away Souvenir Of The
Greatest Day In The History Of Literature

MILLIONS of literature-lovers all over the world spent June 16 2004 reliving, minute-by-minute, the most famous day the world of books has ever known.

Now you too can join some of the world's greatest bores *(Surely "American professors of literature")* as they recreate via the internet every tiny detail of the day that has become universally known just as "Bore's Day".

It was exactly 100 years ago that James Joyce's legendary hero Leopold Bore got out of bed in a Dublin tenement and embarked on the events of the day which has inspired literary scholars ever since.

With the aid of this second-by-second guide, specially compiled for Private Eye by **Professor Arnold J. Pipesucker**, James Joyce Professor of Semiotics at Ithaca University, New Dworkin, Mass., you can follow every episode in the twenty-four hours which launched Leopold Bore into the pantheon of literary immortals.

Bore's Dublin (as it is today)

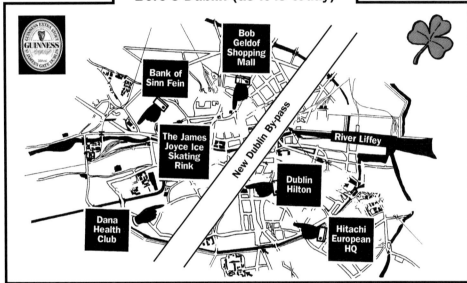

Times And Places – Your Journey Through Bore's Day

8.10am
Bore gets out of bed at 245 Stalegrass Crescent (now demolished and site of Starbucks World of Coffee).

8.35
Bore puts on trousers and discovers one button missing.

9.11
Bore goes out to buy button at Molly's Buttons 'n' Bows haberdashery shop (now site of Phuwhatascorcha [Ireland] Video Games Megastore).

9.51
Bore watches No. 94 bus going by and muses on thoughts of ladies without any clothes on (today the 94 bus route to Ballymoney has been withdrawn from service, but the 81B travels much the same route).

10.36
Bore crosses De Valera Bridge over the Liffey and catches sight of his former schoolfriend, Fergus O'Cash (Bore would have known the De Valera Bridge as the William IV Bridge).

11.15
Bore enters O'Halloran's Bar on Casement Street (now the Shamrock Bistro) where he drinks a pint of Guinness while sneaking a look at the embonpoint of the barmaid Polly O'Worsthorne *(Click on thumbnail to see webcam of Polly's Naughty Night With Her Lesbian Friend)*.

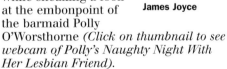
James Joyce

11.50
Bore falls asleep *(So do we. Ed.)*.

9.21pm
Bore wakes up, and walks home via St Stephen's Green (now Vodafone Park).

9.36
Bore notices lost button on floor and muses on mystery of human existence.

10.15
Bore falls asleep (again).

This unforgettable literary experience has been brought to you by Gnome Leisure Enterprises in association with the Arts Council of Ireland, the Irish Heritage Tourist Board, Aer Lingus and the European Union.

THAT BECKHAM PRE-EURO 2004 PRESS CONFERENCE SUMMED UP

"The allegations against me are scurrilous, ludicrous, shocking and lots of other words that almost, but not quite, mean 'false'"

77

WHEN YOU AND THE BAND ARE TOURING THE WORLD DO YOU STILL LEAVE A TRAIL OF HAVOC BEHIND YOU?

WHAT?!

YOU KNOW, TRASHING HOTEL ROOMS, LETTING OFF FIRE EXTINGUISHERS, DRUNKEN BRAWLS, DRUG-CRAZED SEX?

I RESENT THAT QUESTION.

I'M A MATURE ROCK STAR, A MUSICAL ARTIST, LOVE...

NOT A PROFESSIONAL BLOODY FOOTBALLER...

YOUR PR IS SUGGESTING YOU DO A PIECE FOR THE MAIL ON SUNDAY MAGAZINE CALLED "IT'S YOUR FUNERAL".

OH YEAH?

AND WHAT'S THAT WHEN IT'S AT HOME?

IT'S A REGULAR FEATURE WHERE STARS AND CELEBRITIES DESCRIBE THEIR PERFECT FUNERAL.

I'LL DO IT.

SO WHAT WOULD YOUR PERFECT FUNERAL BE, SIR?

ANY OF MY EX-WIVES' I RECKON.

LOVE THE NEW SINGLE, GARY.

THANKS. I WANT TO RELEASE IT NEXT MONTH.

AND I REALLY LOVE THAT YOU'RE GONNA GIVE ALL PROFITS TO CHARITY.

WELL I WANT TO PROMOTE MY ALTRUISTIC SIDE...

SO HAVE YOU THOUGHT ABOUT A TITLE?

OH YEAH

SINCE MICK BECAME 'SIR' MICK I'VE THOUGHT ABOUT NOTHING ELSE...

WHY DO YOU THINK HE'S DOING IT FOR CHARITY?

GARY YOU'RE DOING PRETTY WELL FIGHTING YOUR SUBSTANCE ABUSE PROBLEM...

THANKS, DOCTOR...

BUT YOU CAN'T BEAT THIS THING ON YOUR OWN... YOU NEED PEOPLE YOU CAN CALL ON WHEN THE GOING GETS TOUGH.

I THINK YOU SHOULD JOIN A SUPPORT GROUP, GARY.

SHAKE

I CAN'T DO THAT 'COS OF WHO I AM, DOCTOR.

I'VE NEVER BEEN IN A SUPPORT BAND IN MY LIFE! I'M STRICTLY A HEADLINE ACT!

BAM!

SHOULD SWISS REF BE HANDED OVER FOR TRIAL?

by Our Football Staff **Al Garve** and **Liz Bon**

Saddam Meier

THERE were growing demands last night for the Swiss referee, whose crimes have caused suffering to millions of Britons, to be handed over to a British court.

Speaking on behalf of the victims, Mr Sidney Bonkers, a white-flag-driver from Neasden said, "It is only natural justice that Saddam Meier should face the impartial judgement of a panel of patriotic English Sun-readers".

Gutted

Said Mr Bonkers, "My entire family was wiped out by his decision to disallow Sol's goal, due to the quantity of alcohol we were forced to consume in order to come to terms with our predicament."

"After this horrifying crime perpetrated by this Alpine assassin from the land of the cuckoo clock, many of my friends were left lying in heaps, legless and brain dead."No wonder we want to give Herr Meier a fair trial before we string him up."

"Football's coming home – I'm being deported"

---

10 Tell-Tale Signs To Help You Spot A Swiss

❶ Mad staring eyes
❷ Stupid beard
❸ Black shorts and shirt
❹ Blind
❺ Totally embittered by England's 3-0 victory over his compatriots
❻ Pockets stuffed with bribes from England-hating German arms manufacturers
❼ Eats revolting cheese full of holes
❽ Silly green hat with feather
❾ Constantly whistles "Edelweiss" and "Hills are alive with the sound of music"
❿ Bastard!!!

Reprinted by kind permission of the Sun Newspaper

GRUNTS AND SQUEALS AS SHARAPOVA TRIUMPHS

by Our Sporting Staff LUNCHTIME O'DROOLZ

CENTRE COURT had never heard anything like it. There were 800-decibel yelps of delight and groans of pleasure from the ranks of the world's pressmen, as they realised that they could put a picture of a blonde teenager on their front pages. Their climactic whoops echoed across the hallowed turf, as the sizzling Siberian sex bomb from the land of nuclear nookie stormed her way onto the front pages. "Yes, yes, oh yes!" cried one editor J. Witherow, as he contemplated the display of long legs, blonde hair and all-round corphewwhatalegova *(continued for 94 pages)*

FLAGS OF ST GEORGE

S.B

FRENCH CONNECTION UK FOUNDER IN £50M DIVORCE

You fcuking btchi

GLENDA SLAGG

THE GAL FLYING THE ST GEORGE CROSS ON HER KNICKERS!!?!

■ WAYNE ROONEY!?! Every mum in the land would like to have a spud-faced nipper like Wayne a-bootin' and a-shootin' in the street outside!!?! We'd all be proud to tuck him up in bed with a cup of Ovaltine and a teddy bear in his little arms!?! Night, night, little Wayney, God bless and sweet dreams!?! All together – aaargh!?!! *(You're fired Ed).*

Byeeee!!!

Exclusive to the Daily Telegraph

Bill Deedes A Very Unbrief Life

In which Britain's greatest living journalist remembers some of the famous people who have been lucky enough to meet him over the past six centuries.

NELL GWYNNE

'Princess Nell, the Queen of Oranges', as she was known to the press corps, was one of the most beautiful women I have ever met. She revolutionised the stuffy court of King Charles with her gaiety, her informality and her genuine interest in other people's problems. I met her when I was interviewing her for the Daily Tudorgraph (as it was then), and even though it was more than 300 years ago, I still remember what she said to me, as if it was only yesterday: "Would you like some oranges, ducky?"

OSCAR WILDE

'Oscar the Master', as he was known to the press corps, was one of the wittiest men I have ever met. Oscar was wonderful company when he held court at the Cafe Royal, with his friends Lord Alfred Douglas, Algernon Swinburne and Aubrey Beardsley. It was not widely known that Oscar was a keen cricketer. He once confided in me, "Dear boy, did you know that I bat for the Other Side" – a team with which I was not familiar. Oscar spent his declining years in France, as a result, I am reliably informed, of his failing health. Typically, his dying words reflected the stylish way in which he had lived: "Very flat, this champagne, my dear. It must be from Norfolk".

THE DUKE OF WELLINGTON

Arthur Wellington was my commanding officer at the Battle of Waterloo, some years after I had been his fag at Eton (or it may have been Harrow). Wellington was a great soldier, but rather less successful as prime minister, a post in which I again served under him as Minister Without Portfolio. I remember him asking me one day, "Where have you left your portfolio, you damned fool?". At least, unlike his successor Sir Anthony Eden, in whose Cabinet I also served, the 'Iron Duke' did not wear yellow socks!

Tomorrow: *Lord Deedes remembers meeting Wat Tyler, Alexander the Great and W.G. Grace.*

Nursery Times

Friday, 9 July, 2004

TWINS TO TAKE OVER FAMOUS NEWSPAPER

by Our Media Staff **Raymond Noddy** and **Stephen Glovepuppet**

NURSERYLAND was rocked to its foundations last night by the news that one of its most respected newspapers, the Daily Teddygraph, has been acquired by the reclusive Tweedle brothers, Sir Dum and Sir Dee.

Little is known of the brothers, except that they are identical twins and live in a fairytale castle on the island of Brilleau.

Barclay's Bank

Staff at the Daily Teddygraph were said to be 'delighted' by the news of their proprietors.

"The Tweedle brothers," said one staffer, "are model proprietors. They just stay quietly in their castle, without interfering, and from time to time send over large cheques for us all to live on."

Other insiders, however, are worried that the Tweedle brothers may wish to boost the circulation by changing the paper's traditional character.

Rumoured moves include the dropping of one of the Teddygraph's best-loved features, the regular printing of pictures of Miss Snow White attending premieres, wearing dresses which leave little to the imagination.

On Other Pages

● Why won't Prince Charming marry the ugly sister? by Linda Lee Potty

DUCK & FOX SPLIT – IT'S OFFICIAL

AFTER months of speculation surrounding their private life, Miss Jemima Puddleduck, it was revealed last night, has obtained a divorce from Mr Imran Fox.

Friends of the couple blame the breakdown of the relationship on their different life-styles and the "incompatibility of the duck and fox cultures".

Out for a Duck

Said one close friend, "it could never have worked. Jemima liked the social whirl of the farmyard, whereas Imran liked roaming the world attacking poultry and young lambs".

Recently Miss Puddleduck, daughter of the celebrated financier Sir James Puddleduck, has been squired around the farm by such eligible bachelors as Hugh Grunt, the handsome young pig, and the fish-about-town Mr A.A. Gill.

Jemima's mother, Lady Annabel Puddleduck, said last

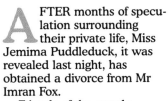

night that she was "very sad" at the break-up of her daughter's marriage.

"But I am sure she will get over it" Lady Annabel continued, "and next time she can do much better than a smelly old fox."

Who Should the World's Richest Duck Marry Next?

You decide. Should it be:
a. **The Hon Jeremy Fisher?**
b. **Lord Peter Rabbit?**
c. **Sir Squirrel Nutkin?**

Ring our 'Lovaduck' Hotline on 08742 620 620 and make your vote count (all calls charged at peak rates, one acorn a minute).

BAGHDAD TIMES

Friday July 9 2004

Nation Celebrates As Democracy Returns To Iraq

by Our Entire Staff **Mohammed Hastings**

SCENES of jubilation all over the country yesterday greeted the historic "handover of power".

Old-age pensioners shot each other openly in the streets, as the sky above Baghdad exploded in an unforgettable display of fireworks, suicide bombs and ground-to-air missiles.

Teenagers joined hands to rush eagerly to the nearest bomb shelter, as helicopter gunships staged a magnificent demonstration of indiscriminate targeted killing.

Sunni Delight

Centrepiece of the celebrations was the ceremonial "handover" itself, when a small group of shifty-looking men in suits gathered under heavy security to read out a statement specially written for them by Mr Paul Bremner, the celebrated impressionist.

The new prime minister of the Free and Independent Democratic Republic of Iraq, Mr Ayad-that-President-Bush-in-the-back-of-the-cab-once, declared, "We, the undersigned, take delivery of one entire country (slightly damaged) and hereby undertake that we will exempt the United States and its allies from any responsibility for anything that happens in the future. Long live Afghanistan – I'm sorry, that should be Iraq."

Mr Bremner then gave his impression of a man running for his life towards the nearest aeroplane.

On Other Pages
Election Latest – Saddam Ahead In Polls 3

"I've got it! We trump up a tale about a beautiful Greek girl, who's been abducted by the wicked Trojans..."

That Honorary Degree Citation In Full

SALUTAMUS PIERO LUIGI COLLINA, REFERENDUM PEDIBALLI INTERNATIONALIS FAMOSUM PER CAPITO BALDICO ET OCULI SWIVELLENSIS, CELEBRATISSIMUM PER SUPERBUS CONTROLLUS LUDI DURANTE TOTALITER XC MINUTIAE (PLUS TEMPUS EXTRA ET PENALTII SI SUNT NECESSARIUS). APPELATUS 'HOMO IN NEGRO', DISPENSOR CARTORUM RUBICORUM ET JAUNUSQUE, SED SEMPER ADMIRATUS PER ACTIONES 'FIRMUS SED FAIRUS' (CONTRARITER REFERENDUM HELVETICUS GITTUS CUM BARBO RIDICULO IN BRITANNICUS VERSUS PORTUGALLUS SCANDALO MAGNATO).

© The University of Hull (formerly Humberside College of Higher Education)

HOW TO SURVIVE A TERROR ATTACK

THE Government's Ten Point Plan to make sure YOU escape the Imminent Holocaust
by Hazel Nuts, MP.

❶ Hide under the kitchen table with your family.
❷ Keep all pets in.
❸ Wear lead-lined trousers or a hat made from asbestos.
❹ Stock up on the following items: baked beans, potato crisps (flavour optional), frozen pizzas and Sunny Delight (fun-pack size).
❺ Don't live in the following areas: Central London, Sizewell B, Baghdad.
❻ Remember that terrorists are still out there trying to kill you.
❼ Which proves that the government were right to mount a pre-emptive invasion of Iraq.
❽ So vote Labour
❾ Er...
❿ That's it.

Nursery Times

Friday, 23 July, 2004

ANIMAL WELFARE LEGISLATION HITS NURSERYLAND HARD

STORIES IN BRIEF

▪ **OLD WOMAN** sentenced to one year in prison for swallowing fly. She asks for spider, bird, cat, dog, and horse offences to be taken into consideration.

▪ MOTHER Hubbard arrested for dog abuse. "Cupboard was bare." says shocked policeman.

▪ **ROYAL CHEF** charged with baking pie containing four and twenty live blackbirds.

"What sort of dish is this to set before the King?" asks outraged RSPCA officer.

"An admirable plan, Mr Gribbs, but short on detail"

Soap Shock

THAT STOLEN EASTENDERS SCRIPT IN FULL

Man: Shut it, you slag.

Woman: Leave it aht.

Another Man: Oi, don't even think abaht it.

Another Woman: We've gotta talk.

First Man: I don't believe I'm hearing this.

Second Woman: You make me sick, do you know that?

Another Man: Shut it, you slag.

First Woman: Leave it aht.

Scriptwriter: I don't believe I'm writing this.

Viewer: Leave it off.

(Continued Episode 94)

Late News

POLICE investigating the theft of six months' worth of *EastEnders* scripts say their greatest fear is that they could fall into the wrong hands.

"We are very worried that whoever has taken them might return them to the BBC, thus allowing the Corporation to film them," said an obviously worried Inspector Knacker.

"We are appealing to whoever has them to hide the scripts under his bed at the very least or preferably to burn them.

"In the hands of the *EastEnders* cast these scripts would be dangerously *(cont. p. 94)*

★ PICK OF THE PROMS

Beethoven's 'Infidelio'

Conducted by **Simon Rattle**
(behind his wife's back)

THE STORY, set in Germany, tells of a beautiful young mezzosoprano who casts her magic spell over the ageing ruler of the Berlin Philharmonic, Sir Simon Love-Rattle. The stricken maestro deserts his wife and runs away with Kozena Fan Frooty, making an aria of himself by singing "Che Gelida Manina" – "My huge bank balance is frozen by my wife".

PAUL FOOT
1937-2004

THE ALTERNATIVE VOICE

with **DEIRDRE SPART** (Co-Chair of the Tufnell Park Stop The War, Smash Blunkett and Save The Slugs Animal Rights Coalition)

Er... once again totally predictably the capitalist media have demonstrated their total and utter contempt for all normal codes of human decency by devoting literally acres of space to the achievements of our Comrade Dave Spart the greatest orator and agitator of our time. What right have these Bush-loving fatcats of the media to express any opinion whatsoever about our fallen comrade whose life was dedicated to smashing the whole corrupt bourgeois fascist system which allows them to exploit the working class er by sitting in the back of chauffeur-driven limousines and stuffing their *(cont'd p. 94)*

Report Into The Absence Of Intelligence On Weapons of Mass Destruction

by Lord Butler of Whitewash

"The main function of intelligence in a post-war period is to think up ways of getting the Prime Minister off the hook"

Claus von Bulowitz

INTRODUCTION

1.1 The remit of my inquiry was to review all the evidence which might have suggested that Mr Blair had done something wrong, and then to ignore it.

1.2 In the course of my inquiry, it was necessary for me to interview a number of distinctly shifty gentlemen whose names cannot be revealed for security reasons.

1.3 Although it was impossible to believe a word they said, I nevertheless decided to give them the benefit of the doubt and to conclude that they were all acting in good faith.

THE EVIDENCE

2.1 Reliable intelligence sources revealed that Mr Saddam Hussein was attempting to buy 240,000 tonnes of weapons grade "yellow cake" from the Republic of Rumbabwe (formerly British Rumbabaland).

2.2 Forged letters relating to this transaction were brought to my attention, but on mature reflection I concluded that they had been forged in good faith and were accepted as such by the intelligence community, to whom no blame should be attached.

2.3 An aerial photograph showing a 'mobile laundry', capable of completing an entire 'wash cycle' in 45 minutes, was mistakenly believed to show a nuclear weapons delivery system, armed with biological and chemical detergents.

2.4 The blurred nature of this photograph made it entirely understandable that this installation was mis-identified in good faith and no blame should be attached to any individual intelligence officer.

2.5 It was reliably reported to London that there were "unquestioned and very close links" between the Ba'athist regime in Baghdad and Mr Osama Bin Laden, head of the Al Qaeda terrorist network.

2.6 These reports were confirmed by a photograph showing two men with beards talking to each other at Prague railway station in what appeared to be a "highly conspiratorial manner".

2.7 I find it in no way unreasonable that this evidence was interpreted by the intelligence services as conclusive proof that we should invade Iraq immediately.

PROCEDURAL ISSUES

3.1 I find it highly regrettable that insufficient memo pads were provided at certain crucial meetings in 10, Downing Street. Such deficiencies would never have happened in my day, when it was considered a top priority that all stationery requirements were supplied in full.

3.2 In my day the following prerequisites were regarded as obligatory at all meetings:

a) **A sharpened HB pencil at every place round the table.**

b) **A pencil sharpener for every four civil servants present at the meeting.**

c) **A Grade One quality India-rubber eraser for rubbing out possibly prejudicial material and inserting the words 'Nothing happened and no one is to blame'.**

THE ROLE OF THE JIC

4.1 It has been suggested that it would be grossly improper to appoint Sir John Scarlett to the position of Head of the Secret Intelligence Service, on the grounds of his perceived failure to identify the distinction between a washing machine and a weapon of mass destruction *(see above)*.

4.2 I have decided on reflection that no blame can be attached to Sir John in this regard, since he was clearly under intense pressure to do what he believed the Prime Minister in good faith had asked him to do.

4.3 No blame, therefore, can be attached to the Prime Minister for his foreword to the JIC Dossier, in which he claimed, in good faith, that Britain was about to be attacked by a nuclear mobile laundry (NML) and that we were all going to die.

CONCLUSIONS

5.1 I find that all concerned in the events which are the subject of this inquiry acted at all times in good faith, even when they did not.

5.2 No blame therefore should properly be attached to any individual, including myself, for producing this shameless whitewash of my old friend and former employer, the Prime Minister.

5.3 Er... that's it.

LORD BUTTERUP

ANNEX A
Members of the Committee

The Rt Hon the Lord Butthead of Beavis KP, KFC
The Rt Hon Michael Condom MP
Field-Marshal Lord Whinge of Singe VD, HGV, TCP, NBG
Mrs Anne Token-Woman MP

ANNEX B

A comparison of the original intelligence reports with the 'Dossier' published by the Government.

What the original MI6 version said	How this passage appeared in the Number 10 Dossier
September 3, 2002	*September 4, 2004*
As yet there does not seem to be any sign of these WMD. But we have one source, Z, who claims that he met this chap in a cafe in Amman who swore that his brother had seen this great big metal tube marked "Weapon of Mass Destruction – Top Secret". Quite honestly, I think we should be a bit cautious about this report, as most of our chaps think that Z is off his trolley.	We now have incontrovertible evidence from a highly-placed and completely reliable source that millions of nuclear missiles containing poison gas and anthrax are fully primed and targeted directly at London, which could be completely wiped out in 45 seconds.

I conclude, from a strict forensic comparison of these two passages, that although significant textual changes had taken place, these were made in good faith and not with any intention to mislead.

Cairo Times

Friday, July 23, 2004

OUTRAGE OVER THAT LONDON MEETING

by Our British Staff LUNCHTIME NO-BOOZE

THE ENTIRE world of Islam was rocked to its foundations yesterday by the shock meeting in London between one of Egypt's most revered clerics, and the fundamentalist left-wing lunatic Red Ken.

The Mullah was seen openly to embrace the world's most notorious homo-phile and pigeon-abuser in a scene which will sicken every decent Muslim the world over.

Statesman and Pariah *(right)*

Livingstone Him To Death

The fanatical British extremist leader has in the past expressed unashamed support for the terrorist group Sinn Fein, and also waged a relentless 'holy war' against London's five-million strong motoring community.

Worst of all, the Red Ken has been accused of violent physical abuse to-wards a practising journalist by pushing him off a wall when under the influence of alcohol, while escorting an unmarried mother at an "immoral and dec-adent" party.

Doing The Islambeth Walk

But last night the respected Mullah Al Qa'eda hit back at his critics by claiming that they had grossly maligned Red Ken in painting him as "some sort of mad extremist".

"On the contrary," said the Mullah, "Red Ken is a moderate voice who is part of the mainstream, and is just the sort of man we have to learn to deal with.

"He is now closely allied to the Blair regime, he is fiercely opposed to trade unions and his pigeon-killing days are long since behind him."

On Other Pages

■ Your Camel Trains Tonight **24**

■ Pyramid-Selling Scandal Exposed **6**

■ Murder On The Nile – Man Held **10**

BUTLER REPORT
Timetable of Events

July 10   Downing Street issues leak saying that Butler Report will be "a bombshell" and that the government will be "rocked to its foundations" by Butler's "damning criticisms".

July 12   Gullible hacks print stories repeating this at huge length.

July 14   The Report appears and is a damp squib.

July 15   Disappointed hacks say it's not as bad as they thought it would be.

July 16   Government is off the hook.

The Prime Minister acted in good faith...

...and I'm a very good actor

Call My Bluff

(BBC1) 1.00pm

That Episode In Full

(Sound of "ping" as word appears on screen)

Fiona Bruce: And the next word is 'Liddle'. Rod, what's a 'Liddle'?

Liddle: Well, a 'Liddle' is a noun meaning the sort of bloke who finally agrees to get married to the mother of his children but then starts carrying on with some totty half his age who he's met at his office. It is a term of abuse really. You might say, "Look at him, what a complete Liddle, I don't want to read about him in the Daily Mail any more".

Fiona: Alan?

Alan Coren: No. No. Rod is bluffing. He's telling you a pack of lies.

Liddle: Hang on, you sound like my wife!

(Daytime audience laughs uproariously)

Fiona: Well, what do you say to that, Rod?

Liddle: Can I have your phone number?

Fiona: Thank you, Rod. Next week's edition of "Call Me In The Buff" comes to you live from the divorce courts.

© BBC Two-timing.

IN THIS WEEK'S BEANO
(Incorporating the Spectator)

Boris the Menace — "CRIPES! HOW ONE OF OUR WRITERS GOT CAUGHT WITH HIS TROUSERS DOWN – AND IT WASN'T ME!"

Rod the Sod — "OOH-ER! LOOK AT THE SIZE OF MY COLUMN, READERS!"

Mini the Skirt — "OLD AND CLAPPED OUT – BUT I STILL LOVE THE SPECTATOR" (SURELY 'MY ROD' ? ED.)

Mrs Liddle — "WHY IS IT CALLED 'THE SPECTATOR' WHEN THEY'RE ALL AT IT?"

IT'S ALL IN THE SPILL THE BEANO!

"Sire, the Gifte Shoppe has fallen!"

PRISON DOESN'T WORK — AT LAST THE PROOF

by Our Prison Staff **Phil Cells**

A SHOCK report by the influential Michael Howard League For Penal Reform dismisses the widely accepted idea that it is possible to reform hardened criminals.

The report cites as an example the tragic case of 'Mr H', a long-term offender, who recently made headlines by announcing that he was "going straight" and that he had learned his lesson.

Horror Tory

"My long years of bitter experience have taught me," he recently announced, "that I have to change my ways and be more caring, compassionate and open to modern ideas.

"Only that way," said Mr H, "can I be accepted back into the community as a reformed character and win the next election."

Back To Smith Square One

But only a few weeks later Mr H was caught slipping back into his old ways.

He was filmed in Middlesbrough on CCTV, shouting "Build more prisons. String 'em up. It's the only language they understand."

NEW TERROR
Vampire Strikes In Broad Daylight

Opera

Stunning new production of Berlusconi's *Il Freebi in Sardinia*, performed by the European Union Orchestra, conducted by Felix Mandelson.

Act One
The young Englishman Antonio, accompanied by his lovely wife Cheriebina, arrives in Italy, looking for somewhere to stay the night. The couple sing the duet *'Nissan Dorma'* (*'We don't want to sleep in the car'*).

Act Two
The villainous Count Silvio appears, disguised as a humble prime minister, and invites the couple to stay with him in his luxurious castle, the Palazzo Cosa Nostra.

The couple are serenaded by the Count's servants, in the famous *Mafiosi Chorus*.

Act Three
Enchanted by the Count's generous hospitality, Antonio sings of his love for getting something for nothing, in the aria *'Dolce fa niente'* (*'It is sweet not to have to pay'*).

But his happiness is short-lived when the local

carabinieri arrive at the castle to arrest his host for not paying his taxes. They sing *'Your bank account is frozen'*.

Antonio and Cheriebina return sadly to Barbados, to stay with their wise old friend Sir Clifford de Riches, who welcomes them with the show-stopping aria *'I am paying for your summer holiday, no more spending for a week or two'*.

DIANA FOUNTAIN FAILURE
Duke of Edinburgh To Blame

by Our Conspiracy Staff **Water Mitty**

AN EXTRAORDINARY new explanation for the persistent technical problems besetting the Princess Diana Memorial Fountain was advanced last night.

According to top fountain expert, Mohammed Al Fayed, the reason the water has failed to cascade in soothing rivulets is because the Duke of Edinburgh has been clogging up the mechanism with leaves. Said Mr Al Fayed, "Every fuggin' night he rides up in his coach and fuggin' four and clogs up the fuggin' fountain with leaves and dead badgers and white fuggin' Fiat Unos, it's the fuggin' truth, he's fuggin' crazy, I tell you."

Diana Memorial Latest

"The pump died"

My eBay

I AWARD YOU THE IRONIC CROSS

YEH, GREAT, WHATEVER

Russell.

Bernard Levin Pays Tribute To The Late Himself

"Where are the songs of yesteryear? Aye, where are they now?"

I CAN only have one subject for my column this week, and that is the departure from this vale of tears – and if you have them, prepare to shed them now – of a man who was most celebrated, as many would argue, and who am I to contradict them, as my Bessarabian grandmother used to say, for his unrivalled mastery of, or some might suggest weakness for, embarking on sentences of such extravagant, nay excessive length, laced, it must be said, with dependent clauses and sub-clauses of such prolixity that they irresistibly brought to mind the operatic works of that unparalleled master, the great, nay immortal Wagner, or, to choose another analogy, the interleaved layers of nectarine and millefeuille served by Monsieur Pierre Grossetruffe in one of those exquisite puddings for which his delightful restaurant Les Trois Pigeons Droles is rightly acclaimed across the known world (and while on the subject, I can scarce forbear also to mention his legendary Bananes de Robespierre) or, to select yet another linguistic trope *(That's enough Levin. God.)*

That All-Purpose Slapper Interview In Full

As seen on ITV and all channels

Interviewer: This must be very difficult for you?

Slapper: I'm still in shock really.

Interviewer: What are your feelings now about *(Here the interviewer may insert the name Sven, Becks, Chazza, Wayne, President Clintstone or whichsoever other celebrity love-rat may be appropriate)*?

Slapper: I always thought we had something really special together. *(Long pause)* I guess I was in love with him.

Interviewer: *(putting on concerned face)*: And are you still?

Slapper *(tears welling up)*: This is very hard for me. I always thought it would last. So yes. *(Camera zooms in for close-up of tears on perfectly made-up face)* The answer is yes.

Interviewer: Join us after the break, when I'll be asking questions about oral sex.

Slapper: Can I have the money now?

(Fade. Commercials for cars, beer, crisps etc. Collage of photos of slapper not wearing many clothes, with caption 'The Slapper Interview – Part Two')

Interviewer: Was he a good lover?

Slapper: Well, I don't like to talk about these things. They're very personal and painful.

Interviewer: Would this perhaps help?

(Assistant producer enters with huge wheelbarrow piled with money)

Slapper: He was an animal in bed. But also very gentle and considerate.

Interviewer: This is more like it! Can you give us a bit more detail?

(WARNING: The following answer may not be considered suitable for family viewing)

Slapper: He ripped off my silk underwear... manhood... pleasure... oral sex... at it all night... best sex ever... always put trousers in trouser press before we satisfied our animal urges... a perfect gentleman...

(Slapper continues in similar

vein until the TV company runs out of money)

Interviewer: Now it's all over, do you feel – how can I put this? – used?

Slapper: No, we were both adults. I went into it with my eyes open. And, frankly, what went on between us is nobody's business except ours.

Interviewer: Thank you very much for talking to us. We'll be sending the rest of the money to Mr Clifford.

(Final collage of Slapper wearing even fewer clothes, counting pile of banknotes)

Continuity: After that historic and extraordinary interview, join us again after the break for the News.

(More commercials for crisps, beers and cars. Followed by News logo)

BONG! *(Or it may be BONK!)*

Newsreader: In an historic and extraordinary interview on this channel, a slapper has given details for the first time of her intimate relationship with a celebrity love-rat.

(Picture of Slapper wearing carefully chosen full-length outfit, possibly white, to suggest to viewers that she is not a slapper, but a put-upon victim of shameless male exploitation. Cut to scene from interview)

Slapper: I went into it with my legs open. Oh no, I've got that wrong, haven't I?

Producer: Can we do that bit again?

© World copyright Max Clifford ITV Slappertrash Productions 2004.

Notes & Queries

QUESTION: What is the longest novel ever written?
Anne Orak, Todmorden.

☐ CONTRARY to popular belief, Proust's *Recherche du Temps Perdu*, at 1,531,216 words, is far from being the world's longest novel. A 19th-century Norwegian clergyman, Pastor Olaf Lurpak, spent 64 years writing a novel entitled *The Saga Of Sven Fjordsmansson,* set between the 8th and 19th centuries, which reconstructs in exhaustive detail the history of a family of fisherfolk who eke a meagre living in the tiny village of Nijsdøn in the Norwegian far north. Lurpak's 20-million-page epic took so long to read that no publisher lived long enough to finish it. The book was therefore never published, but, after Lurpak's death in 1895, the manuscript was carried in 20 ox-carts to a specially-built wooden museum on a hillside outside Nijsdøn. There for some years it was made available to the scholars of the world but sadly none of them responded to the challenge. In 1927, alas, a fire caused by the knocking over of a kerosene lamp reduced Lurpak's masterpiece to four tons of ashes. These were ceremonially scattered by the mayor of Nijsdøn and his fellow villagers onto the waters of the fjord. In 1984 a commemorative plaque, jointly funded by the University of New Dworkin and the Women's Literary Circle of Neasdenburg in Florida, was erected on the site of the former Lurpak Museum and stands there to this day, as living testimony to the astonishing feat of Nijsdøn's industrious pastor and most famous son. *Gabriella Lurpak, New South Wales.*

QUESTION: Why is the Lilo so called?

☐ MRS Rusbridger (24 May) is completely wrong when she informs us that the term 'Lilo' for an inflatable floating mattress was originally derived from the idea of a device on which one might "lie low". The inventor of the Lilo, Ernest Hislop (no relation), took the idea and the name of his invention from a portable bed which he observed on a visit to Tsientsin in the early 20th century. The bed, constructed from bamboo leaves and porcelain, had been designed by the legendary 16th-century monk Li-Lo. Hence the name! Q.E.D. Mrs Rusbridger should do her homework before bursting into print with her ill-informed views! *Edward de Bonio, Isle of Dogs.*

Answers, please, to the following: Do some spiders sing? Who was the first 'Lollipop Lady'?

"I'm not laughing, I was just expecting something a bit more hi-tech"

ATHENS 04

As the eyes of the world focus *(Surely 'close with boredom'? Ed.)* on the greatest festival of the sporting calendar, the *Eye* picks out the six competitors whose feats will soon be the talk of the planet *(Surely 'nobody at all'? Ed.).*

Paavi Nøgud

Six months ago the 23-stone Finnish underwater weightlifter was an unknown health and safety inspector. Today he is poised on the brink of global stardom in the 3-Snatch Freestyle Synchronised Tango (Bantamweight Division).

Jiffie-Lou Goldberg

This 19-year-old jet plane on legs has taken the world of 500-metre running by storm with her spectacular use of performance-enhancing pharmaceutical products. Says Jiffie, *"No one in Athens is going to catch me – I hope!"*

Klaus Boremann

At 93, this former Darmstadt postman could write his name into the record books when he becomes the first man in history to lift gold in the new Olympic sport of dominoes. He may, on the other hand, die in the attempt.

(That's enough 'Six To Watch')

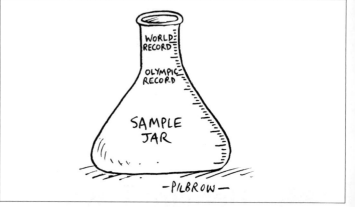

WORLD RECORD

OLYMPIC RECORD

SAMPLE JAR

—PILBROW—

What's So Wrong With Wasps?

Asks The World's Worst Columnist Max Hastings

ON ALL sides these days I hear people complaining of a plague of wasps.

Picnics are spoiled. Barbecues are ruined. One cannot even sit out in the garden, reading a copy of the *Daily Mail*, they say, without being pestered by one of the little black and yellow brigade. *(Keep going. P.D)*

But I ask this. What's all the fuss about?

Are we such a namby-pamby nation of wasp-fearing wimps that we can't cope with a few harmless stings?

I say it's time someone stood up for the Great British Wasp.

What, I wonder, would Winston Churchill have *(cont'd. p. 94)*

(cont'd. p. 94)

© Dacretrash Productions

GREEK OLYMPIC TRIUMPH

GOLDEN TEARS FLOW AS GOLDEN MATTHEW STRIKES GOLD

by Phil Space

AT LAST they came. And there was no stopping them. First it was a slow trickle and then an uncontrollable flood turning into great sobs of relief as journalists across Britain wept openly with relief as at last they had a decent Olympic story to put on the front page.

The stiff upper lip that had held

out all through the badminton and the cycling finally quivered and then broke down in tears of unbridled joy.

Said one blubbing editor, Martin Newboy of the Daily Telegraph, "It's what we've trained for and dreamed of for all these years. And when the moment comes you can hardly believe it. An opportunity to put tearful public schoolboys on the front page of (cont'd. p. 94)

WHY PLUCKY PAULA DIDN'T WIN MARATHON GOLD FOR BRITAIN

Those Theories in Full

❶ **UNFAIR** track conditions organised by corrupt Athenian Olympic officials

❷ UNFAIR weather conditions organised by corrupt Athenian Olympic weathermen

❸ **UNFAIR** pollution cynically orchestrated by Athenian Taxi-drivers over last 80 years

❹ UNFAIR other contestants deliberately running faster than Brave Paula organised by corrupt drug-taking Athenian Olympic gangsters.

❺ **UNFAIR** baseball cap planted on Paula's head by sinister, Athenian/Japanese Triads in League with Al-Qaeda.

❻ UNFAIR weight of expectation placed on Golden Paula by desperate British tabloid sports hacks in pathetic attempt to sell papers. *(You're fired, Ed.)*

LATE NEWS

■ **STRAW** flies into Athens to see scale of Paula Radcliffe tragedy for himself. *(Reuters)*

Love Is Blind

by DAME SYLVIE KRIN, best-selling author of
Heir of Sorrows, and La Dame Aux Camillas

THE STORY SO FAR: It is the night of the Spectator *party – London's most glittering social event where the cream of the capital's political and literary lions mingle with the world's most beautiful women.*

Now read on...

THE ATMOSPHERE was filled with gaiety and laughter; champagne corks popped and snatches of brilliant conversation wafted on the breeze through the gardens of Doughty Street... "Michael Gove is the one to watch" ... "I think UKIP are the real threat"... "They only pay £100 for a column. Worse than the *Oldie*..."

And there on the edge of the throng was the beautiful American heiress Tiffany Cartier, whose father owned most of New Dworkin and ran DworkMart, the rubber-tyre-to-breakfast-cereal conglomerate. Nervously she sipped her glass of Francis Pym's No. 1 Cup, trying to find a friendly face in the crowd who she could approach with confidence.

They were all so sparkling and brilliant. There was Boris Johnson, the dashing young editor, in his bicycle clips, fresh from the House of Commons, who many tipped to be the new leader of the Conservative Party. And at his side the devastatingly attractive columnist Petronella Wyfront, giggling at Boris's every *bon mot*. And there in the corner, under the table – wasn't that the glamorous tousle-haired controversial writer Rod Liddle, surrounded by a bevy of gorgeous young girls from the magazine's sub-editing department?

Standing there in the blossom-scented courtyard, it was clear to Tiffany that romance was everywhere.

But sadly not for her. All her diamonds and jewels, her Puccini handbag and her little black cocktail dress from Schumacher's could not conceal her feelings of loneliness here in London, thousands of miles from home.

SUDDENLY something cold and wet touched her beautiful perfectly-formed thigh. She looked down to see a black labrador. And behind the dog was the most attractive man she had ever come across. And she had seen many at her father's celebrated New Dworkin soirées – Jeb Bush, Donald Rumsfeld, and even Henry Kissinger.

But this man was different. Bearded, tall and distinguished, he had the enigmatic smile of a man who could always make a woman feel wanted.

"What ho, Home Secretary! Jolly decent of you to come to our bash!" boomed Boris, rushing forward with hand outstretched to greet the mysterious stranger. "Let me introduce you to our publisher, the gorgeous Tiffany Cartier. Tiffany – this is The Right Honourable David Blunkett."

The timid American millionairess could scarcely contain her excitement. She gulped. Not *the* David Blunkett? The David Blunkett behind the crackdown on asylum seekers?

"I'm an alien," she said wittily. "I hope you're not going to send *me* home!"

He chuckled. "You have a beautiful voice," he said. "And I expect you are a very beautiful woman."

The floppy-haired editor of the *Spectator* realised that he was in the presence of a chemistry that was growing more powerful with every second.

"Ooh-er! I'd better make myself scarce," said Boris with the subtlety that was his hallmark. "Oh look – there's Oliver Letwin. I must go and commission an amusing Diary from him..."

SUDDENLY they were alone. Tiffany and David. Together. With only Sophie the faithful guidedog as chaperone.

"I think she likes you," said the hirsute Home Secretary. "These dogs guide you down the safest path, but something tells me that the path we're going down together is anything but safe..."

There was a scream of delighted laughter as the dashing figure of Rod Liddle fell out of a window into the goldfish pond.

This was going to be a night to remember...

(To be continued)

© *Sylvie Krin 2004.*

BLUNKETT NEW CRACKDOWN

by Our Home Affairs Staff **Taki Stuff**

THE HOME Secretary has announced a new crackdown on media intrusion into politicians' private lives as "an important part of the war against terror".

Police will be given new powers to arrest on sight any journalists lurking outside senior politicians' love-nests on the grounds that this breaches the vital security of the government.

Reporters who write about politicians' affairs will be subject to on-the-spot fines or even imprisonment "for aiding and abetting terrorists".

"You have until the end of today to leave London," he told reporters "or you will be shot on sight."

"No, dear... only the nappies are disposable"

'IRAQI POLITICIAN NOT CROOK' SHOCK

From Our Man In Baghdad **Rageh Omaar Simpson**

THE WORLD of Iraqi politics was rocked to its foundations yesterday when another car bomb blew up. But there was another story which has left observers shocked and stunned with disbelief.

It has been revealed that a member of the new Iraqi Ruling Council, Mr Ahmed Wannabi, had committed no crimes of any kind, and appeared to be entirely innocent.

Even the most hardened Iraqi analysts were disbelieving that such a thing could have happened.

Said one of them, "We have crawled over his record with a toothcomb, and we cannot find a single case of fraud or even murder".

Mr Wannabi is now being widely tipped to be the next person to be assassinated by one of his colleagues.

On Other Pages

HOWARD PLEDGES TO END POLITICAL CORRECTNESS

I've done nothing correct politically since becoming Tory leader

Nursery Times

.... **Friday, 6 August, 2004** ....

DEFENCE CUTS HIT HISTORIC REGIMENTS

by Our Tin Soldier Staff **Captain Correlis-Barnet**

THE Grand Old Duke of York's regiment has been made the target of swingeing cutbacks in the latest defence review which has reduced the once-proud fighting force to a shadow of its former strength.

Said one military expert, "The Grand Old Duke of York, he had ten thousand men,

but now he's got three and a laptop".

When asked whether he would be marching this new streamlined rapid response unit anywhere, the Grand Old Duke of York said, "Unlikely. Morale is very low. When we were up, we were up, but now we are very down indeed".

That Bob Dylan Honorary Degree Citation In Full

SALUTAMUS ROBERTUS DYLANUM (NATUM ZIMMER-MANICUM) CANTORUM AMERICANUS FOLKERENSIS ET HARMONICA VIRTUOSUM. CELEBRATISSIMUS ANNOS SEXUAGENSIS CUM HITTO MAXIMO 'AVE HOMO TAMBURINUS', 'TEMPORES MUTANDO' ET NATURALITER 'RESPONSUS EST, AMICUS MEUS, PUFFERANDUM IN VENTO'. PER MULTOS ANNOS INSPIRATIO PROTESTORUM ANTI-BELLICUM ET ANTI-CAPITALISTICUM CUM AMICA JOANNES BAEZANTIUM ET CETERA. CONTINUIT CUM SADDO BARBATO ET CAPELLIBUS CURIOSIUS ET INHALANS MARIJUANUS ICONICUS ALTERNATIVUS CULTURUM HIPPIUSQUE. ACTORUS NON MEMORABILIS PERFORMENSIS IN 'PATRICIUS GARRETUS ET WILLIAMUS MINIMUS'. NUNC HABITUS EST IN CROUCHUS FINIS NON-DESCRIPTO SUBURBO LONDINIO. SIC TRANSIT GLORIA MUNDI.

© University of St Andrews (formerly The Glen Miller Distillery and Polytechnic, *"A wee dram afore ye graduate"*)

GLENDA SLAGG

FLEET STREET'S MARATHON MOUTH!?

■ **SHAME** on Wayney! You were the spud-faced nipper who every Mum wanted to tuck up in bed. Now we find that "tucking" isn't what you're after!!?!? You're nothing but a potato-headed sexaholic whose sleazy antics make every mum in the country want to throw up!?!! Go on Roodeney! Buzz off! Your career is definitely on the 'wayne' geddit? He does but only if he pays for it?? Geddit?!?! *(You're fired. Ed)*

■ **COME ON** Mr Pressman!! Leave the spud-faced nipper alone?? He's hardly out of short trousers (well apart from Saturdays) but he's just a teenager with a normal healthy appetite for money and prostitutes!!!??

What red-blooded young man with a few million quid in his pocket wouldn't spend his nights filled with lager giving Chantelle and Michelle a good seeing to down the local knockin' shop!???!

Hats, trousers and condoms off to the future of English football!?! Hip, Hip, Hoorooney!!? *(You're fired. Ed)*

■ **WHO SAYS** 'A' levels are getting easier??! I'll tell you what Mister, when I took 'A' levels, a fail really meant something!!?! And I got three of them!!!?! But it never did me any harm!??!

You know what's more important than G.C.S.E!!??! You guessed it, S.E.X.??!? And I got plenty of that!!?! *(You really are fired. Ed)*

■ **THE SCREAM** – arentchasick-ofit?!!! Ok so it's been stolen. Who cares?? Who would want Mr Munch's misery guts masterpiece hanging on their bedroom wall??!!

Not me!!?! I wouldn't give the Norwegian nightmare a pass at Art 'A' Level!!?!

And anyway, with that on the bedroom wall even spud-faced nipper Wayne Rooney would be hard pressed to keep his mind on S.E.X!!?! *(Right that's it. Clear your desk. Ed)*

■ **HERE THEY ARE** – Glenda's Bonk Holiday Beefcakes:

● **Alfred Brendl** – So you've given your last performance at the Proms??! How about coming round to Auntie Glenda's for an encore??!?

● **Abu Hamza** – How about hooking up with me, big boy!???!

● **Teodoro Obiang Ngnema Mbasago** – Crazy name, crazy dictator of Equatorial Guinea!!!?!?

Byeeee!!!

School news

St Cakes

Pinsent Term begins today. There are 375 oarsmen in the school. R.J.L. Coxless (Cracknells) is Head of Rowlocks. P.D. Cry-Baby (Kleenex) is Chief Blubber. The Departments of Science, Humanities, Languages and History have been replaced by the new Redgrave Rowing Academy under the supervision of Mr D.R. Stroke-Rate. Crabs will be rowed over Sobber's Mile on Nov. 23rd, St. Tissue's Day. There will be a performance of "Four Men in a Boat" in the Ed Coode Hall. Tickets from the Bursar Rear Admiral Sandy Wetbob (Bronze Medal in the Double Skulls at the Berlin Olympics 1936). In and outs will be on Dec. 3rd.

MUM'S DAD'S

Kelly

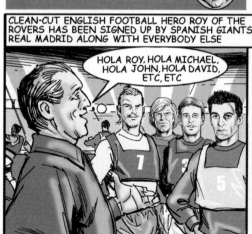

ROY of the REALS

CLEAN-CUT ENGLISH FOOTBALL HERO ROY OF THE ROVERS HAS BEEN SIGNED UP BY SPANISH GIANTS REAL MADRID ALONG WITH EVERYBODY ELSE

HOLA ROY, HOLA MICHAEL, HOLA JOHN, HOLA DAVID, ETC, ETC

THE LANGUAGE IS TURNING OUT TO BE A BIT OF A PROBLEM FOR SOME OF THE PLAYERS

JUGADORES INGLESES DEL FUTBOL! BIENVENIDO AL CLUB MAS GRANDE DEL MUNDO!

LUCKILY ROY COMES TO THE RESCUE

DON'T WORRY LADS, I KNOW ENOUGH OF THE LINGO TO GET BY

SENOR BOSSO! DONDE ESTA LOS NIGHTCLUBS Y LOS PROSTITUTAS?

THREE BEERS FOR ROY!

HOORAH!

COOPER.

MANDELA LEADS WORLDWIDE CAMPAIGN

Don't free Mark Thatcher ♪♪

THATCHER'S ESCAPE PLAN

The desert, and step on it

When a Mother's Love Turns to Grief

by **Dr Charles Moore,** Consultant neuro-Thatchologist at the Institute of the Today programme

However much we admire Baroness Thatcher for her incomparable achievements, bestriding the history of the late 20th Century as she does like a Colossus, there is always a price to be paid for such outstanding success in life.

During the years when she was running the country, her children inevitably saw less of her than they would have done if she had stayed at home, cleaning behind the fridge, reading them bedtime stories from the Daily Telegraph and generally "being there for them".

In the case of her son Mark this failure to carry out her full nurturing role has created a massive guilt complex, and she has over-compensated for her earlier lack of maternal engagement by indulging his every wish.

Such a son has often, as Freud pointed out, turned into an international playboy, when, given a more stable upbringing, he might have secured a proper job such as being editor of the Daily Telegraph, working for a respected businessman like Lord Black.

Today, in the twilight of her years, Baroness Thatcher faces one final terrible humiliation – having to read the biography of her written by myself.

DRAMATIC NON-ARREST OF COUP PLOTTER

by Our Mark Thatcher correspondent **Sahara Sands**

THE MAN behind a hare-brained plot to overthrow a corrupt Third World dictator and install a puppet leader who would grant access to the country's oil reserves has not been arrested.

Squads of armed police failed to swoop on the conspirator's luxury home in the heart of London's fashionable Westminster.

Coo What A Thatcher

The plot for which the non-arrested supercriminal was not gaoled was masterminded by a group of American misfits who in recent years have been responsible for a trail of acts of violence across the world.

Its leader is a Texan former draft-dodger and reformed alcoholic known to his mercenary associates as "Mr President".

His British henchman, the subject of the dramatic non-arrest today, has been often described as "the son of Mrs Thatcher".

Others, however, describe him as "a complete thicko and a chancer on the make".

"The President" and his ruthless cronies have long had their eye on the tinpot state of Equatorial Iraq, ruled for years by a psychopathic dictator.

Dogs of Straw

With its rich oil reserves, it offered a tempting target for a take-over, toppling the dictator and installing in his place a convicted criminal, Mr Chalabi, who would then act as the conspirators' puppet in handing out lucrative contracts to the conspirators' finance wizard, known as "Deadeye Dick Cheney".

The part played in the conspiracy by the British conspirator known to "The President" as "My Little Tony" is mysterious.

Apparently his role in the attempted coup was simply to "do what he was told" and to provide one helicopter.

When Mr Blair failed to appear at Bow Street earlier today, to face a charge of impeachment brought by a Mr Boris Johnson, no one was at all surprised.

Mark Thatcher is 53.

NEW OUTSOURCING SHOCK

by Our Economic Staff **Cal Centre**

THERE was anger last night following the announcement that Britain was to be closed down and moved to India.

Said a spokesman for Britain, "In today's global environment we simply cannot afford to stay in this country. By relocating Britain to India (just outside Bangalore) we will be able to provide the same services at a fraction of the cost."

Norwich Union Jack

But British citizens were angry at the move which could cost 30 million jobs. Said one, "I tried to complain about this but I was put through to a call centre in Madras."

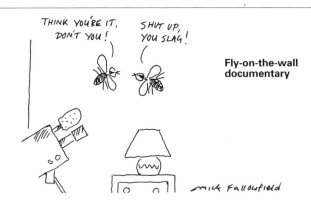

THINK YOU'RE IT, DON'T YOU!

SHUT UP, YOU SLAG!

Fly-on-the-wall documentary

mick Falloufield

Love Is Blind

by DAME SYLVIE KRIN, author of
La Dame Aux Camillas, Born To Be Queen, You're Never Too Old
and thousands of other romantic best-sellers from the Gnome Airport Collection

THE STORY SO FAR: Beautiful American heiress Tiffany Cartier has fallen in love with the tortured but deeply masculine Home Secretary, David Blunkett. But can their love survive in a cruel world?

Now read on...

"HAVE THERE been any messages?" Tiffany Cartier shimmered into her oak-panelled office at the world-famous *Spectator* magazine, and looked expectantly at her young personal assistant Henrietta Starborgling-Smythe.

"Yes", Henrietta smiled back at her perfectly-coiffed American boss, "three hundred – all from Mr Blunkett".

Tiffany sighed sadly, as she looked around the room, which was decked from floor to ceiling with bouquets of red roses and expensive boxes of chocolates from Slater and Walker of Bond Street.

"Who sent all these?" Tiffany asked, knowing only too well in her heart what the answer would be.

"They're from Mr Blunkett too" Henrietta giggled.

Tiffany sat down wearily in her elegant Chipperfield chair, crossing her perfectly-formed legs in that way that over the years had driven so many middle-aged men wild.

"How long can this contine?" she mused, as her gaze wandered over the draft of a new subscription offer, which promised the chance to win a free lunch at the Garrick Club with the magazine's legendary editor Boris Johnson.

But Tiffany somehow could not focus on the mundane details of the business world.

Her mind and every thought returned to the man who for three years had made her life the most glorious romantic adventure she had ever known.

There had been their first encounter at that star-studded *Spectator* party when their eyes met across a room crowded with all the most famous faces in literary and political London – Oliver Letwin, Sir Peregrine Worsthorne and Greek shipping magnate Taki Takealotofcokeupthenose.

Then there were their idyllic, oh-too-short weekends at the hunting lodge on the Chatterley estate, so kindly lent them by David's friend, the Duke of Derbyshire.

How they had laughed when the kindly old duke had dropped in one day with a

brace of pheasants, quipping "One good pair deserves another" as he gazed appreciatively at her exquisite embonpoint.

Later the 89-year-old had paid her the finest compliment the English aristocracy could offer when he confided to David, "if you ever get tired of her, old boy, I wouldn't say no to a shot at her myself!"

How she loved the English with their old-world courtesy and well-bred charm – so different from the callow and brash New Dworkin millionaires who had once queued for her favours in the days when she was fresh out of Vasseline College.

PERHAPS THE most wonderful memory of all, however, was that unforgettable holiday, when David had whisked her away for a few days to the romantic Greek island of Intakos, the birthplace of Venus according to the local tourist office.

How she had blushed when they signed the hotel register "Mr and Mrs Smith", and the cheeky receptionist had tapped her nose and said "You no worry. You have nice time, Mr Blunkett!"

And later, as they strolled along the beach in the moonlight to the distant strains of a local fisherman singing a love song as he strummed his 8-string *balaklava* (or was it a *bazooka*?), David had whispered in her ear that it was time for a crackdown on benefit fraud.

They were all alone under the murmuring olive trees, except for David's Home Office minder, Sergeant Heffer, and David's faithful guide dog Hazel, who kept trying to ruin the romantic mood by growling jealously whenever David put his arms around Tiffany's alabaster shoulders.

She closed her eyes, and could smell again the fragrant blossom of the rumpipumpi trees and could hear the chorus of cicadas and the gentle lapping of the...

"CRIPES! Sorry old bean!" It was the tousle-haired editor, Boris, bursting in unannounced to disturb his publisher's reverie.

"I should have knocked really! Never know what might have been happening in here! Ha, ha!"

His lascivious chuckle and unwarranted innuendos seemed to make a mockery of her high-flown romance.

"It's not like that between David and me", she protested bitterly, feeling the tears welling up in her eyes.

"You wouldn't understand the meaning of real love".

The member for Henley looked sheepish.

"Alright, Tiffie old thing, no need to throw a wobblie. I only looked in to check on what was happening with those bulk copies we're dishing out free on Equatorial Guinea Airlines".

At that moment a leather-clad motorcycle courier was ushered in by Henrietta, clutching a giant pink teddy bear from the Giles Brandreth House of Bears.

A hand-written card proclaimed for all to see the message "I can't *bear* it without you".

The editor's heartless guffaw rang right down the corridor to where the Associate Editor Ron Liddle was enjoying a quick midday "siesta" with one of the girls in the marketing department.

But how would it all end? Tiffany wondered helplessly as the rain lashed the windows of the ancient building and the grey clouds rolled across the darkening sky.

(To be continued)

© *Sylvie Krin 2004.*

Why I Say Blair Should Be Strung Up

by Boris Beano

Cripes! Crikey! We've got a great piece in the Spec this week (not about you-know-what, nudge, nudge, wink, wink!). Apparently, according to this Welsh Johnnie, there's a jolly good chance of impeaching Blair for telling a whole string of big fibs about the Iraq war and WMD and all that malarky.

What a brilliant wheeze, say I! I mean, there's no doubt at all that Blair is a complete rotter, and his pants are on fire most of the time. And if they aren't, they jolly well should be!

Not that I'm against the Iraqi war! Don't get me wrong. No, Blair was 101 percent right on that one. I backed him all the way. Saddam was a totally rotten egg, and it was quite right to go in and biff him for six.

So let's not hear any more of this tommy rot about impeaching the prime minister. Crikey, what a stupid idea. *(Reprinted courtesy of the Daily Telegraph.)*

"Compensation... compensation..."

GRAUNIAD

University Courses Still Available

University of the South Circular (formerly The Polytechnic of the A205)

BA (Hons) in Bus Texting Studies

A three-year module on the social role of text messaging from overground public transport facilities with particular emphasis on the upper deck.

The Ikea University of South Wales (formerly KFC, Newport Pagnall)

MA (Hons) Graham Norton Studies

4-year diploma in Norton iconography with reference to influence on the lexicon of mainstream broadcasting. Sandwich course.

The University of Sellafield (formerly Windscale Polytechnic)

BSc (Hons) How to Work Your iPod.

A seven-year vocational course on the practical operation and functionalisation of *(That's enough courses. Ed.)*

"We're the only ones who've failed"

EXAMINATION BOARD

BUSH ATTACKS KERRY

This guy has made things up about the war to make himself look heroic

And that is *my* job

The Official Report into the Leaking of the Hutton Inquiry Report to The Sun

by Lord Hutton

WHILE it may be true that when reading his advance copy of my report Alastair Campbell may subconsciously have given the impression to everyone working in Number 10 that it would be in the Government's interest to leak my report to the *Sun* by jumping up and down and screaming "The stupid bastard's only gone and cleared us!", "We've got Gilligan and Dyke by the balls!", "Those BBC bastards are going to pay now!", and "Trevor Kavanagh has to see this now – not in 45 minutes' fucking time!"... I found no evidence whatsoever that anyone in Government was responsible for leaking my report.

Therefore I conclude that it must have been done by Andrew Gilligan... or Greg Dyke... or one of those other evil BBC people.

NEW INHERITANCE LAW SHOCK

by our Tax staff **Lou Poll**

THE Government's new proposals on inheritance will deliberately penalise high-earning middle class professionals, it was claimed yesterday.

Critics say that the new legislation will mean that, for example, a fifty-year-old scotsman who is looking forward to inheriting a prime London property in, say, Downing Street from his ageing Prime Minister, may never be able to enjoy the benefit. Said the Chancellor of the Exchequer, "I've worked all my life to get into Number Ten and now this stupid inheritance law will make me so unpopular that it'll never happen."

He continued, "Why is this government attacking the very people who it should be rewarding, i.e. prudent, thrifty caledonians like myself?"

HM Government

PREPARING FOR EMERGENCIES

A Personal Message To All Householders from The Rt Hon David Blunkett MP.

HOMEOWNERS

When a copy of this leaflet falls through your letterbox it is VERY IMPORTANT that you should not be worried.
DON'T PANIC.

The purpose of this leaflet is to warn you that at any moment you may be the victim of a terrorist outrage.

What Will It Be Like?

At the moment we cannot specify, for security reasons, the nature of the threat which is facing us all.

- **It could be a 57-megaton nuclear device landing in your garden.**
- **It could be a deadly nerve gas seeping under your door or coming up through your drains.**
- **It could be a swarm of deadly killer bees swooping through your loft window or catflap.**

But it is very important to keep things in proportion. It is vital that, on reading this leaflet, you should not be alarmed or panic..

ARE YOU PREPARED FOR THE HOLOCAUST THAT COULD BE WAITING JUST AROUND THE CORNER?

Here are some essential steps which every householder must take to survive the death threat from beyond.

❶ Food

It is vital that you stock up with sufficient food for you and your family for what could be years.

Recommended items include:

- **24 sacks of flour**
- **12 crates of Pot Noodles**
- **400 tins of Baked Beans**
- **16,000 cans of lager (brand optional)**

DO NOT FORGET YOUR PETS. They too will need feeding!

(Remember: It is an offence under the new Animal Rights Act to expose your pet to starvation during a national emergency. Goldfish excepted.)

❷ Other Essential Non-Food Items

Ensure a plentiful supply of warm blunketts and torch batteries.

- **One petrol-driven generator *OR* 2-megawatt wind turbine on roof.**
- **Tin opener**
- **Shampoo** *(as this may become scarce as the earth disintegrates).*

(SUGGESTION: This pamphlet, which is printed on recycled paper from sustainable forestry, can itself be recycled to make the equivalent of ten sheets of luxury toilet tissue.)

❸ How To Keep In Touch With The Outside World

In the event of the world coming to an end, you should keep your radio or television set tuned in at all times, for further instructions from the Emergency Powers.

If you are for any reason unable to read this pamphlet, copies are available from your local town hall in the following languages:

Gujerati, Urdu, Estonian, Etonian, Malibu, Rumbabese, Maldivian, Salami, Cornish, Clotted Cream.

Copies in Braille may be downloaded from the Internet.

This leaflet is also available in cassette form from www.werealldoomed.gov.uk

IMPORTANT

This leaflet is only intended as a guideline to assist you in preparing for the catastrophe which we are predicting could happen at any moment. Whatever you do, don't panic and do not spread alarm among your neighbours.

© D. Blunkett, Wasteofmoney Productions 2004.